Dreams and Reflections
COLLECTION

SCHOOL OF DESIRES

Reflections 2

ALSO BY SYLVIE GENDREAU
Published by Céra

City of Intelligences
Rumors of the Future Collection — Essay

School of Desires
Reflections 1
Dreams and Reflections Collection
2004

SYLVIE GENDREAU

Photographs and Drawings
Pierre Guité

SCHOOL OF DESIRES

Reflections 2

Translated by Robert Majzels and Erin Mouré

Dreams and Reflections
COLLECTION

To the memory of my parents

D E S I R E

B E A U T Y

D R E A M I N G

ESCAPE FROM REALITY

Infinite desire

"It's the dreamers who change the world, the others have no time."

Albert Camus

1

In the airplane on the way back to Montreal, I thought of Hubert. I saw us once more seated in my favorite tearoom, whose gradations of pink, gold and chestnut brown gave it that cozy French feel that tourists seem to enjoy.

For my part, it reminded me of holidays, because I stopped there from time to time on days off or while shopping on Place de la Madeleine. It was a place to meet my friends. I went there alone too. Seated in a quiet corner with a book, at a time when the crowds were busy elsewhere. Sometimes the book was just a pretext, lying on the table in front of me, while I daydreamed.

How can you not associate such a tearoom, all pink with shelves full of pastries, with childhood celebrations? I enjoyed watching the elderly ladies with their little dogs and the children (of every age!) gaping at the cakes.

The contrast with North America was great. The customers of the tearoom reminded me of characters in the Countess of Ségur's novels I'd read as a child.

I think I'm better at idling away time in cities other than my own. I observe in silence, with a foreigner's eyes. I can sit in one place for hours. It's quite relaxing to hear the silence, to let one's gaze alight on objects that normally wouldn't attract attention. Very small ordinary things.

That day at noon, he was slightly late and, as a result, slightly tense. Of all my French friends, Hubert is the funniest. He's a poker-faced guy whose quick-witted repartee always makes me laugh. This time was no exception.

He'd barely caught his breath before he started in, showing me that he hadn't lost his touch in the decade since we'd last met.

In his closely fitted suit, his cravat and his serious look, he seems the picture of sobriety. Suddenly, out of nowhere, he cracks a joke. Always on the mark, and sharp and witty.

That day, he was radiant. His eyes shone as he told me that the beautiful Senegalese woman with whom he was in love was now living with him in France.

I knew he'd been in search of a great love after an amicable break-up. I was happy to see he had found it. It was just one more proof that desiring was worthwhile. Dreaming.

We talked about my collective intelligence method and the difficulty that men have with sharing power. He told me that, as a psychologist who offered personal coaching to senior managers, he often used a candle metaphor to help them see power differently.

"A candle," Hubert said, "loses none of its flame when it lights another." I smiled.

Now, as the plane taxied along the runway, a ray of sun that had entered the window and come to rest on my hands reminded me of that candle metaphor.

With half-closed eyes, my head resting against the pillow, facing the window, I thought about light. And how it energized me.

I often wonder how people who live in lands where darkness reigns six months of the year manage. I wouldn't have thought to compare power to a flame, but the idea was not far-fetched.

Collective power is always stronger when intelligently channeled. But it can be detrimental as well: I thought of the failure of communism and other social movements that treat humans like sheep, depriving them of the ability to think for themselves.

Those who try to keep the whole flame to themselves end up getting burnt. The problem is that such autocrats, in their thirst for glory, power and capital, can annihilate entire populations and countries before their madness is stopped.

I recalled the aversion of both Hermann Hesse and Stefan Zweig to movements of mass delirium, both of them having seen Hitler at work haranguing crowds.

The plane was lifting off. I opened my book, thinking of what terrible things fear and stupidity could make men do. I was reading *The Joke*, by Czech novelist Milan Kundera.

He plunged me into the absurd and artificial world created by a totalitarian party. The degree to which a person caught in such a collective insanity can become mistrustful of others is mind-boggling.

Once more, I felt how urgent it is that we learn to think for ourselves. Today the madness of Islamic extremism threatens, but its origins are no different than those of all the other totalitarian and mind-numbing follies of the 20th century. It's far less exotic than we think, and no more barbaric than what we are capable of in the West.

If we could admit this, we might be inclined to fight more intelligently to preserve our freedom. Or at least more humbly.

We certainly won't achieve anything by waging war or by placing power in the hands of a few demonical leaders who treat good and evil as black and white. What pretentiousness to think any of us could be absolutely free of evil! We all have our share of it within us.

In the name of good, such people embody stupidity. But aren't there too many of us who keep silent? Doesn't silence make us complicit?

By now, my seat was bathed in a blinding light. It was too much. I lowered the blind. A little light had satisfied me; too much sent me looking for shade. It made me realize the importance of contrasts. The danger of too much light was not unlike the danger of too much glory, too much power and might.

Hence the importance of proportion to maintain a balance, the importance of the movement between light and darkness, of creating space between oneself and others, and the importance of varying rhythms between exhilarating speed and the slowness that refocuses us. I had always thought of myself as someone who needs light, but suddenly I understood that I needed my share of darkness too in order to move on. It was thanks to the dark that I was able to find a middle way, a measure of balance.

I knew that the way to wisdom lay through acceptance. Even as a child, I had had trouble accepting injustice. My questions to my mother were an unending string of whys. Why ugliness, why disease, why poverty, why suffering, why misery, why war?

Why? Why? Like all children, I wanted to know the why of everything, but I had an unreasonable obsession with the dark side. My mother, a very pious woman, could offer the occasional answer, but never enough to satisfy me.

How can anyone reply to questions that are beyond answers? As an adolescent, coming to grips with the world, I realized the absurdity of a certain type of religious discourse. I couldn't understand how adults listened to such ideas without protesting. It seems I was not alone in thinking this way since, in Quebec at least, the churches have been mostly deserted since that time.

I still had faith, and have to this day. I'm more of an agnostic than an atheist. I feel no allegiance to any sect, and I believe most organized religions are nothing more than sects. I understand the need to gather together, the importance of symbols and rites. If I didn't I could not have developed my collective intelligence approach.

But when people lose their critical judgment, I worry. Unfortunately, it seems we lose it fastest in a crowd. As a result, I'm always wary of large gatherings, especially when they are combined with empty speeches.

As for the Catholic religion, that of my parents, I was rapidly angered by its refusal to accept women and by the lack of evolution in its discourse and thinking. I do not find the threat of hell after death very credible, when we do so much to create it right here on earth. At this time in my life, I have a strong desire for coherence.

My attraction to the light has nothing to do with the religious movements that have been at the origin of so many wars. It's simply been there, for as long as I can recall. Like a fact.

There's a part of me that works hard to protect my innocence, an openness awakened by the slightest contact with poetry, beauty or goodness.

I have not lost that child within me, and I try to leave her sufficient room to dream. I owe my freedom to my dreaming.

But what drives me forward is always the desire for beauty rather than the fear of ugliness (or of hell, as some would say). It seems to me that to motivate people to act out of fear only reduces them to childishness.

That morning, confined to my airplane seat, I realized that I preferred a ray of light to a blinding beam.

I made a parallel with love and happiness. I'd always wanted to experience great love, great happiness, great challenges.

Right then, though, I realized that depth of feeling could be found more readily in subtlety than in the grandiose.

The friend who had just accompanied me to the airport in Paris had compared happiness to a web to which we add tiny touches of color every day. A few hours later, in mid-flight, between two clouds, I understood the meaning of what he'd told me.

I had always wanted huge changes, great improvements in the world, but now, at last, I understood that this made it hard for me to appreciate the value of those small touches that many of us add each day to the great web that is the world. There had to be another way of looking in order to better design the future.

I felt the need to reshape my gaze to see the wonder in all things.

Where does charisma come from, that quality of some people whose mere presence captivates us? I'm particularly sensitive to the beauty some people seem to radiate. My mother was one of those people. Her mere presence lit up a room, made you want to live, to sing and to laugh. In her company, a kind of energy seemed to radiate from one person to another, like light.

The opposite can also happen: depression can spread and infect everyone with the blues. **We are influenced by our surroundings.**

That's why moderation is so important. Too much euphoria is no better than too much depression. In his book on happiness, the Dalai Lama discusses this balance, this acceptance, this happy medium integral to Buddhism. I heard and understood it, but I had great difficulty in applying it on a daily basis. Passion is creative. I was afraid that, if I became too balanced, I'd lose my creative impulses. A bit of revolt and anger can also unleash fine creation.

The flight was going well, without much turbulence. The blinds were down; the half-darkness had calmed the passengers, who had finished their meals some time ago. Some slept; others watched the movie. I could hear the distant murmuring of the attendants. I enjoy that moment of a flight when everything becomes quiet.

During this flight, I'd realized the importance of the give-and-take between possible and impossible.

I'd understood that by letting time pass between movements, we could better attain that middle way where everything becomes possible.

I owed this wisdom to a tiny ray of sunlight that had come to rest on my hand.

A flash of understanding.

I recalled the words of my friend the writer Michel Random, in *The Transpersonal Vision*: "To be victorious," he writes, "we must act from within; the subtle and the qualitative end up triumphing because they carry the power of life within them." After all, "a system is just a system,"[2] he adds. So there's no reason to accept defeat.

Although I knew the initial battle must be waged from within, it always seemed easier said than done.

"… Any awareness," Gaston Bachelard explains in *The Poetics of Reverie*, "is an increment to consciousness, an added light, a reinforcement of psychic coherence. Its swiftness or instantaneity can hide this growth from us. But there is a growth of being in every instance of awareness. Consciousness is in itself an act, the human act. It is a lively, full act. Even if the action which follows, which ought to have followed or should have followed, remains in suspense, the consciousness-as-act is still completely positive or kinetic."[3]

My solitary journeys were good for me. They were moments conducive to dreaming. I rarely took out my laptop, and was content with a notepad and book.

Some of my most innovative ideas had come to me while traveling, as had some moments of great lucidity, of coming to terms with things. These moments were both fleeting and intense, as is dreaming in general.

In *For the Love of Art*, Régis Debray writes: "Time spent daydreaming is the most conducive of all to transforming reflex into reflection. Those hours we think of as empty are really our strongest moments, when we become productive because we're doing nothing."[4]

The airplane began its gradual descent. Bit by bit I came out of my dreamlike state, put my books and notepad away in my bag.

In a matter of minutes I would be in the arms of my beloved.

Traveling without luggage, I was the first out of the plane. I passed through Customs with a wave, and the large doors opened. My partner was there waiting for me, with his beautiful smile.

The joy of reunions, rediscovering the other person, even after seventeen years together. Homecomings are always wonderful moments.

Each time, I'm sad to leave him, but I cherish these absences of ours, because of the pleasure of reuniting. Because of desire, which never diminishes.

Some beauty in the world may escape me, but I've always heard the call of love.

For seven years now, I've been living in my dream apartment, a perfect place for daydreaming.

I designed my home as a monument to idleness. I envisaged it with eyes closed, before it even existed. In my life, I've achieved several dreams, but I've chosen to tell you about this one because it's so concrete. Perhaps it is more apt to convince the skeptics of modern times.

As a girl, when my father told me: "You have to accept your lot in life: you weren't born with a silver spoon in your mouth"; I replied "Don't worry, one day I'll buy the silver mine and there'll be plenty of spoons for everyone." Yet I'm no business whiz either. But it was inconceivable to me to start out my life with such narrow and confined possibilities.

I couldn't believe that fate could be that much of a straightjacket, even before I'd tried my hand at anything.

Unbeknownst to him, my father had done me a great favor that day. He'd given me the drive to desire, the will to dream and the strength to act.

From that moment on, I knew I wouldn't do it just for me, but for my beloved parents too. By broadening my life, I could broaden theirs as well. Knowing this gave me greater strength. I wanted to prove to them that we could determine our own fate, and win the privileges of princes. Nothing less.

That was the beginning of my intensive waking dreams. Many have come true; some have yet to be achieved. My apartment was one of those dreams. Sadly, my father was no longer alive when I bought it. Now I feel that I accomplished one of his dreams. For her part, my mother was amazed. To her, the apartment represented one more step in that pact I had made with them at the age of thirteen. For many years that pact was the seed from which sprang all my desires.

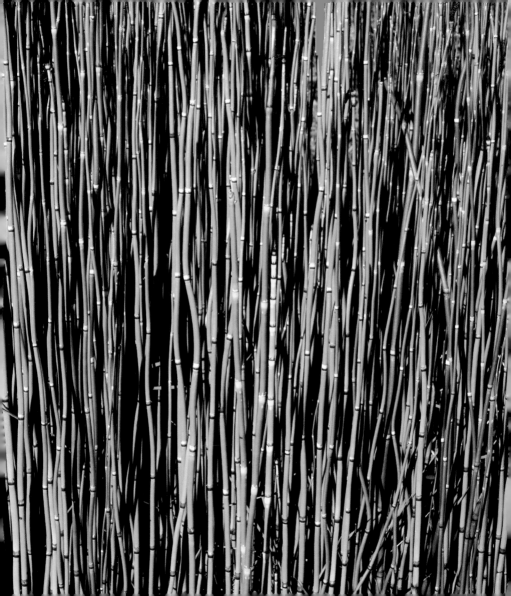

My apartment constantly reminds me of the presence of the marvelous in my life.

Its history, like any story of a dream come true, is magical. It's been said that you only have to desire something for the universe to conspire to help you get it. I think this was one of those cases.

It began on a summer Saturday. We had taken a walk in Old Montreal, then gone in to see an exhibition at the Pointe-à-Callières Museum and stopped for tea on the outdoor patio of the top-floor Arrivage restaurant.

It was dusk. A gentle breeze swept over us and the enchanting view of the river. I turned to my sweetheart and told him that my dream was to someday have an apartment with a view like this.

It seemed highly improbable to both of us. But it was fun to talk about it. It was a dream. Or rather the beginning of one.

In the months that followed we didn't mention or think of it again. Until Christmas day.

We'd taken my mother to Notre Dame Basilica. It was a tradition she always enjoyed. The morning was bitterly cold; the thermometer had plunged to –40°. Bundled up and huddled together, the three of us walked quickly down the frozen sidewalks back to the car. Even the sun and sky seemed frosty.

Our pace slowed at the sight of a new housing project on Rue de la Commune, facing the river. We stopped to peek through the fence surrounding the building site.

I thought, some of those apartments will have a view of the river like the one we admired last summer from the patio of the museum restaurant. "Lucky devils," I said to myself.

Winter and spring passed. I forgot about it. Walking in Old Montreal with my mother near summer's end, we happened on the site again.

The concrete skeleton was now covered. The apartments were already up for sale. I visited every one of them, or rather their sites, to find the best view.

I let my interest be known, though I didn't have the money to buy one yet — especially since my ultimate dream was to buy two of them, one to live in and one as an office.

I went to see the banker. I said, "I have a dream." He replied, "Money talks," and told the developers not to take me seriously.

I was just a dreamer!

Visiting the apartment at dusk, I'd noticed a string of small blue lights along the river to guide maritime traffic. They might have been stars floating just above the ground.

Several days later, I bought a doorknob in blue Murano glass, the same color as those lights along the river. I carried that doorknob around in my purse like a charm, showing it to a few close friends as I told them about my dream.

Everyone came up with ideas to help me raise the money. It was great.

During the following days and weeks, I sketched the plans for my next apartment on tracing paper. Every night, I fell asleep within the walls I'd dreamed.

It seemed impossible for that apartment to belong to anyone but me. It was my dream.

Potential buyers who had shown interest before me backed out. When I was at last able to make an offer, I found the money for the deposit. I could think of nothing else.

My dream surprised me because, until I'd turned thirty-nine, I had never had the desire to own property. I wanted to remain free to go where I pleased. The acquisition of property seemed like an albatross, an unnecessary weight.

But this time was different. I was under the spell of that river view, that corner of the sky, that old neighborhood. After the first victory, we found the energy during the following months to carry out enough contracts to make the next payments.

Everything was coming together as if by magic. There was a fascinating synchrony, as though the universe was conspiring to help us; doors opened of their own accord.

At the time I'd negotiated the purchase, the apartment was only a concrete shell, which meant I was able to complete it myself step by step and according to the plan I'd dreamed for months.

Though I wasn't an architect, I found craftspeople willing to support my project. I scribbled my ideas down in sketchy diagrams; we talked them over and, gradually before our eyes, my dream took shape. It was fabulous, a creative project.

Everyone was complicit: from the agent Louise L'Heureux, to the developers and all the trades-people who contributed to this collective construction.

The quality and originality of the final result are eloquent proof of what collective intelligence can create.

My sweetheart hadn't wanted to become too involved. He thought my dream too ambitious, and worried I'd be disappointed if the project fell through. He supported me, but discreetly. As for me, I pursued my dream like a dog gnawing a bone. All my energy was focused on achieving it. Since then, whenever I tell him I have a dream… there's a moment of silence. It would never occur to him to laugh, however, no matter how improbable the dream might seem.

That's why, whenever I come home to Montreal after one of my long absences, my apartment symbolizes more than a roof over my head. It represents the memory, the embodiment of the achievement of a dream that seemed impossible at the start. It embodies the hope and energy that make me want to continue dreaming.

I love every nook and cranny of this place, which was designed as a jewel box for the river and sky.

That's the only reason I fell in love at first sight!

I wanted to live with the feeling that the floor of my house is an extension of the river and the walls are part of the sky. That was the absolute dream.

Even after years of experience with waking dreams, I'm still moved each time the magic works.

As a child I would go to bed early, so that I'd have time for a bit of reverie before I fell asleep. I invented part of my life in those reveries. When I was still young, during my idle moments, I dreamed of the free and autonomous woman I wanted to be.

I dreamed I wouldn't have to live the way my parents did. I believe I've succeeded. I dreamed of a great complicit, complementary and reciprocal love. Of all my dreams come true, this one is the most precious. If it were to end some day, I would be happy nonetheless and grateful to have lived a beautiful love that helped me to grow within.

Naturally I have dreams that have yet to be realized,
but I'm not done yet, nor am I done dreaming.

The waking dream is a key that gives me access to a universe that would otherwise be closed to me. It's the key to my desires. On sad days, I dream so as not to die. On thinking days, I dream to live. Dream to invent. Dream to design. Dream to see differently. Dream to create. Dream to act. Dream to love. The waking dream is my eternal accomplice, the first step to a multitude of possibilities.

To me, desiring doesn't mean I'm constantly dissatisfied, and take refuge in dreams to escape reality. Rather, it means brief daily flights from reality so as to constantly reinvent my life with the help of those creative drives — my desires and dreams.

For me, dreaming is spiritual gymnastics, a plunge into the imaginary that lets me match images to my ideas and link all I see, sense, hear and desire. Dreaming allows me to invent.

"Imagination," as Italo Calvino defines it, "is a repertoire of potentialities, hypotheses, of things that are not now nor have never been, and may never be, but could have been."[6] Recalling Giordano Bruno's *Spiritus Phantasticus*, in which he describes "a world or container of forms and appearances that is never saturated," Calvino adds, "… I believe that all forms of knowledge must draw from that container of multiple potentialities. The mind of the poet, and the mind of the scientist at decisive moments, works by associating images, in a process that is the fastest system for linking and choosing between the infinite forms of the possible and impossible."[7]

It seems to me that, if there were more of us dreaming while awake, this container would be even richer. Instead, these days, it's almost exhausted. How can we dream when experts claim to do it for us? How can we dream when we have no free time? How can we dream without moments of inactivity? Without quiet strolls?

The great danger that threatens us is our excess, our bulimia. Too many images saturate our imaginations. Too much music silences us. We don't sing anymore. Too much noise deafens us. Please, can't we have a moment of silence? Let there be a little mystery to awaken our imagination.

Apparently, more and more children suffer from problems like insomnia, because there's too much noise. People go deaf at a younger age.

From my apartment, the view is not as beautiful as it once was. Streetlights were installed too close to each other; they cast a blinding light that obliterates the stars from my corner of the sky. It's time, urgently, to freeze the frame. Beauty is in danger!

I want to take a few minutes every day to start again. To empty my mind. Italo Calvino wanted to warn us "of the danger of losing a fundamental human faculty: the ability to see clearly with our eyes shut, the power to produce colors and shapes out of an alignment of black letters on a white page, the aptitude for thinking in images."[8]

Imagination is our greatest personal and collective natural resource. It's a resource as important as the environment and requires our attention.

This is a call to everyone: let's close our eyes to see more clearly. We must look after our desires and dreams. Then we'll see what we can accomplish by assembling the creations of our collective imagination. We are influenced by our surroundings.

The quest for beauty is everyone's concern. We must be moved by it. All of us, without exception. So that each person, when deciding something in relation to their job, will think differently and choose, for example, streetlights that cast a gentler light toward the ground, and then place them further apart.

Meanwhile, someone else, organizing a concert, will tone down the amplifiers just a bit. We need to learn to strike a balance, to find the happy medium. It's the art of living, an art of beauty that goes against the trend toward mega-everything, against the need to think big.

We need to dream while joyfully accepting our limits or, as Montaigne put it, "take honest pleasure in our being." Young people take inspiration from what we adults do. I was able to dream at such a young age, because my parents granted me those moments of idleness and dreaming, those moments of silence. Some evenings my father would sit me down beside him and say, "I've got a lottery ticket in my pocket. What would you do with the money if we won?" That would kick off a wonderful evening of dreaming and discussion that kindled a heartfelt desire to create and share, even before I possessed anything.

My parents taught me that acceptance did not have to be passive. Constraints could become, depending on one's viewpoint and perception, a hormone that triggers urgency, and the adrenalin to produce imagery.

Some days, a guerrilla band of desires can push us to create; at other times, a calm serenity allows us to rest. Life is a multitude of moments in the present. Like us, it changes, vibrates, twists. Life is movement.

When we analyze reality, we freeze it. But, in fact, it never stops; it's in constant motion. As René Lenoir writes, "movement is not created from the identical, but from the new."[9]

What makes for better concentration? Better inspiration? Do we find answers more easily when we've articulated our desires? Do we perceive our surroundings differently when we're conscious of our desires? Does our relationship to the world change?

As soon as I pay attention to the ways things are woven around me, my questions multiply. From time to time, I string events together to end up with extraordinary stories. People say that magical things happen to me, but I think it's the same for everyone, except that we rarely take time to analyze details and link our desires, our dreams, our will, our disappointments, our successes and our failures.

To me, life is a tapestry we weave each day with the threads of our surroundings. Our gaze, along with the gaze of others, determines what pattern will be created. Some synchronicities are too striking to be ignored. Reading a book, for example, we find that the author is speaking of things so important to us that we have the feeling he or she is responding directly to our questions. Individual events can take on special meaning, depending on our emotional state at that moment.

At some other time, the same event, book or film, will have a completely different effect. And what about truly major encounters, the kinds that seem to change our lives. Love, friendship, professional projects — everything intertwines. At times, it's as though there's a kind of collusion between us and the universe, between our desires and our life as it takes shape.

Nature, fashion, the media, public places all nourish the collective unconscious from which each of us constantly draws. It provides us with the signs we're looking for, depending on our attitude, our state of mind.

If you're trying to design a set for the theatre, for example, ordinary objects will seem to call out to you. If you're working on a novel, the slightest street scene may set you off on a new plot development.

"… To let chance intervene is to take a step back from our mind's habits, to abandon our interventionist tendencies for a while so that other signs can appear in which we can read analogies between what we perceive and what we don't," Pierre Faure explains. "By attending to such signs, we are not concocting doubtful interpretations based on blind intuition, but are letting ourselves create descriptions that allow us to break free of the narrow point of view in which we were imprisoned."[10]

We are constantly making up stories out of our own and other people's lives. Our memory retains certain facts, and our brain fills in the blanks to tie everything together. According to recent scientific research, especially in quantum physics, the reality we perceive is the creation of our own mind.

If my brain creates reality, it's obvious that, for me, desire has always been creative. I'm not one of those people who won't let themselves dream or hope out of fear of suffering.

I may sometimes fall hard, after such small disappointments — and there are necessarily many of those — but my ideals always spring back, like young sprouts making their way through hard ground or rock. I need utopias so I can move forward. If I can't see the possibility of a better life, a better world, I immediately feel like I'm spinning on empty.

Which doesn't mean that I don't appreciate living in the moment. Let's just say that I appreciate it more when I have the sense that I'm living it with all my senses and participating fully in making it, through my dreams, my mind and my acts.

Shouldn't we give young people the opportunity to desire? By fulfilling their wants instantaneously, aren't we killing their desires and even their need to desire? Aren't we crippling their ability to dream while awake, and stunting the development of their psychic powers?

I have no idea where this way of clinging to an ideal comes from; I only know that I've always had it.

It must be a child's conviction buried deep inside me. And a way of finding meaning by linking my personal desires to utopias. The method is far from Cartesian, but it yields surprising results. It's as though I used the stuff of my desires to fashion landscapes in my imagination, which then became real. I can't explain it but, thanks to this process, I've always believed everything is possible.

In fact, it's a child's game I've never given up. Why give up an activity that affords me so much pleasure?

Some people see life as a struggle. I prefer to see it as a game and make my choices accordingly.

"The child that doesn't play is not a child, but the man who doesn't play has lost forever the child who lived in him, and he will certainly miss him," poet Pablo Neruda writes in his memoirs.[11]

Even in our era of disdain for utopias, I believe it's essential to hold to our ideals. In fact, I made this the basis of my seminars on leadership and creativity. The workshops thus became a context for sharing my questions with others, putting our thoughts together, and especially for experimenting with new approaches so as to better understand the processes of collective creation. We did so without any illusions about clarifying the mystery of creation, knowing very well that knowledge often brings more new questions than real answers.

We can take inspiration from those who have struggled through difficult childhoods, and yet succeeded in transforming their pain into foundations for building their lives. In *A Marvelous Misfortune*, Boris Cyrulnik explains that "… almost all those who survived developed, very early on, a theory of life that fuses dreams and rational thinking. Almost all the resilient children had to answer two questions. The first — Why do I have to suffer so much? — pushed them to reason. The second — How will I be happy in spite of everything? — incited them to dream. When this inner determinant of resilience was met with a helping hand, the future of these children did not lack promise."[12]

"When they were offered a helping hand," he writes. Food for thought. Are we sufficiently open to offer our fellow beings a helping hand? Are we sufficiently present to the world?

For each of us, life is either a struggle or a game that teaches us to learn and to invent ourselves. Antonio Negri goes so far as to argue "Life is a prison when we don't create it."[13]

It's a heroic struggle, as Michel Lacroix reminds us. "In primitive societies, one reached the status of adult through a series of initiation tests. In all civilizations, the hero who willingly faces danger is the one who attains full self-realization."[14]

Let's awaken our desires, dream our lives. Let's rediscover an ideal. Is the game that hard?

And if we aspire to belong to a civilization worthy of being called by that name, let's stop venerating victims. Let's spur each other to fully realize ourselves by becoming aware that we all have imagination, if we are willing to give it the quiet and stillness it needs to come to the fore.

This is a call to everyone. Let's dream the world, multiply beauty. Let's escape from reality, for just a few minutes a day, to take the time to recreate it.

This was my dream, that summer. And summer was drawing to a close. The air was cooling off. Summer would soon slip away and autumn would be knocking at our door. To my relief, it was quiet once more beneath my windows. But my life was about to become hectic again.

Montreal, August 2002

THE DREAM'S SHARE

"If Humanity accomplishes more than mere existence, it will not be the result of action alone, even the most beautiful and exalting actions; it will come, rather, from the contemplation that precedes actions and must follow in their wake."[1]

Gilles Vigneault

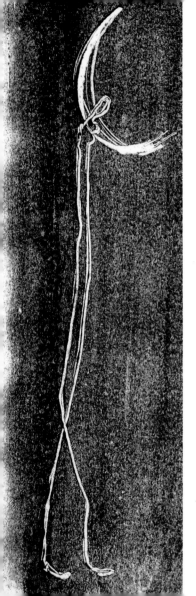

2

For two years, my life had not felt inspiring. It seemed to me I had to take new risks to widen my horizons. I had been responding politely when others requested my collaboration, but out of concern for others rather than in harmony with my own desires.

Saying yes with my head while my heart said no was making me look gloomier by the day. My smile had vanished. I was becoming downright glum.

I felt boxed in by jobs that no longer sparked any passion in me. Some days the world seemed a complete disappointment. Money wasn't enough of a reason for me to keep going in this way.

Eight months earlier, I'd advised one of my clients that I would be leaving them. The date was almost there. I knew I had to make some major decisions before I turned my anger against myself.

More than ever, I wanted to construct a life in harmony with my desires.

Although the next four months were full of journeys back and forth between Montreal and Paris, and other local trips, I knew the end was coming and would bring me a bit of calm and freedom to consider my desires.

Often, on gray or rainy days, the Internet brought me surprises. Now, as I sort my notes, I realize to what extent the pages of my variously colored leather-bound notebooks are interspersed with email from readers. I'd printed the most beautiful ones and pasted them into my journal when I received them. They share space with my daily notes.

As I write this book, I reread these old journals and rediscover the wonderful messages from readers thanking me for *City of Intelligences*, which, they tell me, keeps them company in their moments of difficulty.

I'm grateful to them for their responses, because they make me feel that I'm bringing just a little light into the world.

It gives me a feeling of being useful, especially on those depressing days when I think our era is on a downward slide.

When I see bodies paraded past us in vulgar fashion, hear coarse language, notice the lack of respect toward others and toward nature, or read in the papers about the popularity of pornographic TV shows during prime time, I admit I feel out of sync with the times, that I'm swimming against the current and, really, am utterly useless... I feel as though I'm from another time.

I'd feel very lonely without my readers and their messages. People of all ages write me to say how much my book comforted them. I want them to know that their responses comfort me just as much.

They are the living proof that the *School of Desires* could exist one day, and that it could help us to behave with greater nobility, compassion and poetry. No, I'm not alone.

My readers make me want to do my best in my profession of being human, to realize my full potential, just as they seem determined to do.

On good days, I'd tell myself that, if there were more of us, we could accomplish almost anything. And when I thought that, I was all the more convinced of my decision to withdraw from the world for a while to write for my readers again.

But to do this required preparation. You can't just suddenly pull back from the world when you're a freelancer. And, indeed, my decision surprised several clients. It's true that it's strange when someone as active as I am announces that she's calling a halt.

We live in a time when short retreats are rare. We're not used to hermits anymore, to their way of life and their quest.

My partner, on the other hand, immediately understood. He told me, "You want to create emptiness around you so as to return to what's essential, like in a Chinese painting."

My client (and good friend) Isabelle also understood. She wrote me: "It's wonderful; you make me think of a bird who's been sitting a long time on a branch, and can finally fly away."

I only had a few more months to hold steady. This gave me a feeling of lightness and, though it may not have wiped away the shadows under my eyes, it gave me back my smile.

It was already a good beginning.

Stealing the invisible. In my creativity workshops, I sometimes ask participants to close their eyes. Not for long. Barely a few seconds, just long enough to take a break from reality, to pause and forget violence, war, poverty, stupidity, noise, over-consumption, speed, the over-blown.

Some do it; others seem afraid to absent themselves this way. But I insist. It's my act of sharing. My way of opening my book of secrets to them. Because, for me, this is a real key. It's the first step toward wakeful dreaming.

My eyelids closed, I take flight into an imaginary world… I invent tomorrow. I'm not sure exactly when the unreal changes into reality. What I do know is that bits of my imagination become, a few years later, parts of my life.

That's why I try to get seminar participants to play my games, so they too can feel the power of their imaginations.

Some days it's reality that seems to be transformed into the unreal, into the imaginary. I feel compelled to understand this coming and going from real to imaginary, and back from imaginary to real, although I know full well that a part of the unknown will always remain beyond my reason's grasp. Not all things are lightness and joy.

I have neither recipes nor answers. I'm simply a companion who allows herself to be as surprised as the participants.

More and more, I enjoy exploring shadows, reflections, twilight rather than light. I feel as though I see more clearly there, just as on days of blazing sun, we search out the shade to escape the brutal glare and regain our sight.

In our modern society, we are bombarded by images. Virgin space is increasingly rare. What will happen then to our dreams and imaginations?

"Originally, my idea for *The Human Comedy*," Balzac wrote, "was like a dream, one of those impossible projects one caresses briefly and lets fly off; it was a chimera that smiled, showed its feminine face then spread its wings to rise into a fantastic sky. But this chimera, like so many, became reality; it had its commands and tyranny to which I had to submit."[2]

A creativity workshop has to deal with this quest for shadows and the imaginary in order to encourage participants to submit to their chimeras. Consequently, I'm sometimes obliged to say things that sound strange, because they intertwine emotion and reason, abstract and concrete, letting-go and the will, visible and invisible.

Why this mixture? Maybe it's because life has a way of mixing up the things we try too hard to unravel. Maybe it's because we want more than little cubbyholes, job titles, well-defined roles, fields, and segmentations that we've built into systems and forms of thought.

Maybe because, after two hundred years of hyper-rationalism, we can feel it cracking at the seams. Or maybe we just need to create a bit of disorder in order to discover the patterns and human musicality that exist behind the chaos.

I don't know the why of things. I've simply signed a freedom pact with myself, determined to let the ideas and questions that come into my head (and my heart) emerge. I have a desire to become more and more of a nomad carrying only my questions about life, dreaming, the unconscious, happiness, passion, the intellect, conscience, apprenticeship, experience, power, the world…

But no answers! Maybe a few intuitions. As though the mere act of sharing my concerns might reveal hidden signs I never imagined were there. It's only at the end of a workshop that I can tell if my strategy has worked, if the magic happened.

As you can see, I speak my mind freely, opening a dialogue in the hope of finding some clarity, without claiming to have a winning formula to offer people. Rather I offer impressions and the occasional minor revolt, because a passionate nature doesn't change overnight.

"I for my part," writes Carl Jung, "prefer the precious gift of doubt, for the reason that it does not violate the virginity of things beyond our ken."[3]

This unusual approach was born on the day that a kind of chaos began to inhabit me. The spark was the death of my mother, my love.

The days and weeks that followed her death, I had experienced grief I never imagined possible. Slowly, doors of fragility swung open to reveal new questions, powerful intuitions and rifts.

At last, all my certainties crumbled, leaving me in a state of confusion where solid ground seemed to have turned to quicksand beneath my feet.

I'd entered a black hole. I scarcely knew who I was. My heart was in anguish. I wasn't sure of my desires or destination. I wanted too much one day, and nothing the next.

This was more than my usual self-questioning; I was calling everything into account, even my right to exist, and all the love and friendship of those around me could not shield me.

It wasn't a depression; I was simply suffering from the absence of someone I loved deeply. I felt as though, in my pain, I experienced the metamorphosis described by Kafka, which brought out all my inner demons that I'd never known. Not all things are lightness and joy.

Three years had already passed since that winter. I'll never forget my quick business trip to Paris, barely four days. My book was not out there yet; I had no apartment, and knew hardly anyone. I'd been feeling a bit down for the last five months.

After a long walk one rainy Sunday afternoon in February, I sat down in a small theatre on l'Île St. Louis, my clothes still soaked from that dampness that goes right to the bone. As I shivered in the dark, Nietzsche's words washed over me like a salve: "It is inner chaos that creates a dancing star."

The deep voice of actor Marc Zammit, reviving all the poetic essence of Nietzsche, accompanied by a chorus singing Latin chants a cappella, or by the pianist Alain Kremski, sounded like a hymn to life to me that day, sparking a ray of hope that entered my heart to the core. At last I felt I could live.

Whenever life sends me such signs, I grow a little humbler. I feel the limits of my will, and it's as though I'm receiving a string of mysterious glass pearls carrying some alchemical message whose meaning I would love to know better.

In other words, I can't explain why, but those four days in rainy Paris somehow warmed my spirit. I felt better at last. In hindsight, it was almost a premonition because, a few months later, Paris would become a very important place for me. At that moment, I did not suspect it.

I don't know if you have had the same experience, but it often happens that a person — unbeknownst to them — answers exactly the question on my mind at that exact moment. It's fascinating each time it happens.

Signs, it seems to me, rarely come when we expect them, but they often come when we really need them.

Personally, the most beautiful signs come to me through the arts, poetry and nature. Of course, you have to be ready to listen, because they are sometimes so discreet that it seems they only want to be heard by vulnerable, sensitive beings.

It's as if a certain fragility can open up a way of knowing immanent in each of us, but that refuses to be revealed unless that fragility is present.

As if the key that unlocks the door is the humility that any difficult journey brings us.

In fact, we all have the potential to listen, but a life full of bustle, too focused on appearances, performance, profit and the latest technology, can sometimes make you lose touch with yourself, can deafen and blind you.

It's easy to see how my ideas can seem incongruous in a conference or seminar when I'm addressing, for example, representatives of an equity capital company that plays daily with the extremes of surplus and scarcity.

What are we expected to believe? That, after progress, it's technology (meaning communications tools) that will solve our society's ills and help us create the one global village? I have my doubts.

I'm constantly surprised by some assertions and how little reaction they provoke. In an article in *Vanity Fair,* a producer with Time-Warner claimed that, in today's world, distribution channels in themselves are more important than content. "The power of the guys who make the 'product' is at a low ebb." Distributors, he explained, are now more important than creators in the marketplace, so it's normal to pay them more money.[4]

And here I am, putting so much importance on creators! How sad, I thought.

A few months later, the Internet company AOL purchased control of Time-Warner. Before our incredulous eyes, we were sliding into a society that ties the fate of creators inexorably to distributors.

While I was worrying about the effects of this corporate marriage on the quality of content and the independence of creators, alarmed about the risk of uniformity, the loss of objectivity, and the lack of a healthy distance between business interests and content, all the talk around me was about mega-bucks for a mega-deal.

Whether we're talking about the information society or the knowledge society, both are in the pay of the same mega-society of capital. Just like a human being, this transaction holds both good and evil. It opens both to great possibilities and to the worst nightmares.

I say great possibilities, because it could allow wider distribution of content that would generate new forms of democracy, increased access to knowledge, more information sharing, sites for collective creation, real interaction between cultures, greater access to education for a greater number — I could go on.

I say the worst nightmares, because it could engender more trivia, poor quality, manipulation, abuse of power, mad races for money, and an unquenchable thirst to control and own everything. Sadly, the number of reality shows and pornographic series on TV already indicates that we're heading in the direction of decadence.

Of course, between these two extremes, there are all the nuances that we'll sketch on the canvas we call possibilities. Whether we like it or not, and even if we would at times like to distance ourselves from acts we abhor, this great work is, in part, ours.

The merger of AOL-Warner is only historic because it was the first of many. Others followed, to the drumbeat of aspiring conquerors attracted by mega-power. They've become the new heroes, modern-day cowboys who've traded in their six-shooters for dollars.

Success belongs to those who know how to move fast. We know this. The problem is that, when you move at such dizzying speed, it's nearly impossible to think of tomorrow. We live in a perpetual state of emergency. We think of now, here, right away, and often we couldn't care less about the consequences for those who will come after us.

Our relationship to time is instantaneous and our need for wealth, insatiable. We've never been so well equipped to communicate, and we've never communicated less. Communication becomes an instrument for its own sake, to the point of forgetting relationships with others and, as a result, the relationship to oneself.

For several years now, we've invested so much hope in the promise of technology that we forget to think of content quality.

Technologies are supposed to be tools for creators, but they mostly serve merchants who, inebriated by profits, will distribute anything as long as they can rake in money.

By distributing such poor content, they think they can numb our minds, so as to make us believe in their communications utopia and forget about the danger to democracy that they represent, with their mega-structures and new centralized powers.

And yet, Armand Mattelart has warned us: "At the core of techno-utopias is managerial thinking, which makes the world increasingly unintelligible by emptying it of what's at stake and who's pulling the strings. It's the end of all active participants except one, the manager, who abdicates all responsibility because the situation is global."[5]

However, a growing number of us are concerned and asking questions:

What will the next millennium look like?

What will happen to schools and companies?

How far will the war of mega-mergers and the race for profits go?

What role will our political bodies play to control global oligopolies, and the megalomania of some leaders?

Will we be the victims (and the designers) of increasingly powerful and manipulative marketing?

My head was full of questions. I was happy to have stopped all my activities, because I didn't want to play a part in a life that ran counter to my convictions, even though I had no idea what I was going to do from now on. I only knew that I had to respond.

Each of us, as producer, consumer, actor and spectator in turn, participates consciously or unconsciously in our collective life.

One way we could increase our participation might be to develop our ability to anticipate. Already, many of us share the same doubts. Who among us has never thought, however vaguely, of the importance of bringing peace to the world? Who has never worried about the kind of society we are leaving to our children?

By sharing our uncertainties, we are already agreeing to participate in the debate. Though our voices may not count for much in the balance, we might dare to ask if the violence in the entertainment media is polluting our children's imaginations, and ask if the mega-companies, who have more influence than all governments put together, will agree to reduce their profit margins to really protect the planet, and respect life and human beings.

We might dare to ask why there are so many suicides in rich countries. And speaking of the rich, how long can we tolerate the existence of extreme poverty without reexamining ourselves? How much longer will money be our god? Will we have the courage to give ethics the importance it merits? Will democracy evolve? How might we improve the way we live together?

I wanted to hear answers from many people, because I was convinced that ideas for improvement would come out of a new kind of communication, a more collective thinking.

We have the ability to envision the future but, paradoxically, we tend more than ever to root ourselves in the here and now, to the detriment of any desire to build the future. We are, yes, condemned to navigate between a fatalism that's both necessary and wise, and a voluntarism that encourages action and building the future. We have to find a happy medium.

Our loss of desire and our fear of tomorrow are understandable. So many questions about humanity's future are more complex than ever. There's a fine line between, for example, the promise of benefits from biotechnology and genetic engineering and the fear that these powerful tools will fall into the hands of unscrupulous individuals bent on power and control over the destiny of peoples.

Such individuals did, do and will exist. Happily, so will their opposites. And even good intentions can have devastating results, or quite the opposite. Not all is lightness and joy. "Evil needs to be pondered just as much as good," C. G. Jung explains, "for good and evil are ultimately nothing but ideal extensions and abstractions of doing, and both belong to the chiaroscuro of life. In the last resort there is no good that cannot produce evil and no evil than cannot produce good."[6]

Too much certainty is a dangerous thing. No one has a monopoly on good or truth. Let's be careful. And humble. The third millennium can bring us the worst, or the best. Anyway, life would be unbearable if we already knew its outcome. Uncertainty, the quest, and the road are the spice of life. Life is a grand creative project.

From that viewpoint, aren't we fortunate to have the chance to create something good?

Between flights, the flurry of meetings and the flood of conference calls, I had a mad desire to participate better. Even if I didn't know how, I was sure that my daily activities were a piece in the puzzle of the future.

Our lives are links in a chain, and the quality of these links will contribute to the quality (or lack of quality) of those who will come after. We're all linked. Those who came before us, and those who will follow.

The desire to build the future is also the taste for invention. My desires trigger the urge to create, even though I know I'm not inventing anything; I'm revealing, reorganizing, interpreting. I feel that everything is there, latent beneath my feet. I am influenced by my surroundings. If I work well, little by little the photograph will appear. I'm just the solution in which it's revealed.

My desire to build the future in no way detracts from my pleasure in the moment. I love the present moment; I let myself be thrilled by the unexpected. I love signs, encounters that become new friendships, and teach us something new about ourselves. Through the other I am revealed to myself. And the other is revealed through me. That's the beautiful complementary nature of love and friendship.

At the same time, I'm curious to see what I cannot yet see. I agree with Edgar Morin "…that our spirit is still profoundly underdeveloped, as are our possibilities for knowledge,

thinking, consciousness and even our affective possibilities…
If a larva can become a butterfly, why couldn't we be capable
of a similar metamorphosis?"[7]

The desire to build the future is linked to this desire to
transform ourselves, this wish to strengthen our ties to nature,
to the invisible and between peoples. In the metaphor of
the butterfly, I see the possibility of a new unity in plurality,
in a harmony never heavy-handed, one that leaves room for
differences. I sense a certain lightness in being what I am and
letting the other be what he or she is. It opens the possibility
of a beautiful complementarity.

Authors like Antoine de Saint-Exupéry are exceptional people
whose poetry has helped us to live better. There are others, of
course, who have distinguished themselves, not through the
poetry of love, but through the venom of hate: Hitler, Stalin…
to name but two. It's up to us to choose our side.

I think, on the other hand, that we are perfectly justified to ask ourselves what this flower of evil is, this drug that drives man to assume the place of a god and decide the fate of others. We know that joggers who push themselves cross a threshold where their body secretes endorphins. They get high on running. What do those who exercise too much power secrete?

If only each of us could awaken our senses, re-appropriating the power of our life and becoming fully present, we could perhaps create a more intelligent and more magical world together.

But for that to happen, each of us must first agree to shed our old skins and search for the nectar that will give us wings instead of cutting them off. Such a nectar would be a wisdom-potion that integrates good and evil, life and death, suffering and happiness, a balancing point to help us better take on life's trials and accept the shadows, knowing that light will chase away the darkness.

If a larva can become a butterfly,
why couldn't we be capable of a similar metamorphosis?"
Edgar Morin

The situation is urgent, because the questions we will be facing in the near future are even more complex than the preceding ones. What consequences will our decisions have on future societies? Does the desire to be cloned, for example, correspond to a desire to be eternal?

"We have to draw the line at cloning," some say. But how can we even think it out fully, if we only act in the moment, abandoning our powers to state entities, whether political or economic?

If we're continuously manipulated by marketing, so that we lose our critical sense; if we're trained in the school of profit until we lose our ability to think; if we're constantly rushed so that we have no time to create what some think of as superfluous or useless — poetry for example, that futility so essential to the human soul — what will become of us?

I say this knowing that there'll always be poets and artists to make us dream and to help us see the beauties of the world that otherwise can escape us.

My intention is not to pass judgment on modern societies, but rather to invite a collective reflection on their buried potential.

This is not a call to return to the past, but simply a warning. By stressing profits and mere utility, we dry up the rich source of modernity, which has already brought us many advantages. Couldn't we benefit from scientific and technological advances, while also developing a new world consciousness?

Why are reason and emotion always presented as extremes? Why this Manichean thinking? To imagine tomorrow: this is the mental game I'd like to invite you to play. What kind of society shall we dream up? Which qualities do we want to develop?

The brain projects its inner perceptions onto the world, and its perception is stimulated by the very actions it's preparing to carry out."

Alain Berthoz

"The brain is not a reactive machine, it's a proactive machine that projects its questions onto the world," writes Alain Berthoz in *The Brain's Sense of Movement*.[8] Science reassures us when it tells us that our memory serves more to anticipate the future than to recall the past. But it does not give us an instruction manual. The quest for the invisible is in our hands.

To explore the invisible, we must learn to see from within. This is no mean feat. We would be wise to heed the advice of Thierry Gaudin, who suggests we avoid Nasreddin Hodja's mistake of searching for his keys under the streetlamp just because it was light there, when he'd lost them at home, where it's dark.[9]

Seeing from within means accepting to explore day and night, which are both aspects of ourselves. Seeing from within means taking inspiration from different degrees of light to awaken the entire range of emotions. We need different ages, different nationalities, different identities to see clearly.

We need many differences to counter uniformity. We especially need many emotions to counter the domination of reason and of materialism which, pushed to the extreme, become absurdities. We must be wary of certainties and quick judgments.

To learn to see requires a demanding consciousness, a continuous awakening. It's an impossible task to do alone. To initiate the movement, we must pay more attention to those who see from within. Then, the noise of this strident society would become less deafening. Unfortunately, in the past, we have often preferred to kill such people. From Socrates to Gandhi and Martin Luther King… we haven't learned much.

To question what makes no sense is often more disturbing than to keep living with foolishness. We find it easier to abandon the sites of public debate to triviality, while telling ourselves that we're becoming a knowledge based society where content will make a difference. But what exactly do we mean by content?

Our sensitivity is shriveling, as is our understanding of complex phenomena. Will we lose our depth under the manipulation of marketing experts? By putting too much emphasis on rapid learning, are we turning knowledge into fast food? In a sea of information, what deserves our attention? It will require a degree of vision and consciousness to navigate intelligently in the third millennium.

"Human beings draw their grandeur from the ability to imagine the future and turn imagination into reality,"[10] Thierry Gaudin says. If that's the case, why are we waiting to act? Let's feed our imaginations and invent a great chain of dreams to transcend this rationalist and capitalist universe. Otherwise, it's just too empty of meaning to be bearable for much longer.

Utopian, you say? Perhaps, but I put more faith in human utopias than in the material kind.

Evolution will not come from computers, nor from distribution channels, but from the vision, intentions and heart of those who dreamed and designed them.

I still have full confidence in women and men even if, sometimes, in the face of so much blindness and manipulation, I feel mute and powerless. I only know that together we could dream and find the gestures that will let us invent a different place.

Speaking at the premiere of his film *La Cena* at the Montreal World Film Festival, Ettore Scola declared: "The restaurant has become the only place where discussion is still possible. As we approach the end of this so-called century of communications, we are no longer communicating…. We have neither the time nor any place to talk. In the past, grandfathers would tell stories at home. Young people could learn where they came from. They knew their roots. Now, only the TV talks. The only place where we can still have a conversation is the restaurant. At least there's no TV there."[11]

The Dream's Share

I would like to turn these pages into a *trattoria* of all nations, eras and disciplines so that, over a good meal, we could converse eclectically on a host of subjects, on life and on the future, to finally build a future. Shall we gather round the table?

For several years I'd been inviting people to take time to wander now and then, to rediscover their freedom, to defend human values that seem important to them, to dream and share their dreams, and, especially, to create, alone and with others. But I felt that this alone wasn't enough.

I had a few ideas about what could be done, but I didn't know what more I could do, for my part, to contribute. A book perhaps. A few seminars or talks. It still seemed insufficient to me.

Questions filled my head. And the more I thought about them, the more they multiplied. No answers came to pierce the fog as I struggled in vain to advance.

The only valid answer seemed to be the force of numbers. Each person had to take up the collective intelligence approach for themselves to give it life.

It could not depend on just a few people. For it to work, it would have to become a great wave, carried onward by all those who believed in it. Not as followers, but as individuals who assume responsibility for their lives and develop their leadership and creativity based on who they are and what they can contribute to others and society. The wave would be one of autonomy, channeled toward a common goal, thanks to the bond of creativity. I imagined new communities emerging across the planet.

Such communities would be without structures, so as not to fall back into our old bureaucratic errors and make everything inefficient all over again. This was, and remains, my great dream. But some days, I felt I was a million miles from attaining it. I saw myself as a Don Quixote, talking for nothing, or almost. These sorts of ideas and values can't be imposed. They have to be chosen and lived by each person, authentically.

People sometimes talked to me as though the collective intelligence approach were mine. I resisted.

I have nothing to sell. All I have is a conviction to share. Afterwards, everyone does what they think is best. We are all influenced by our surroundings, but we are also free beings. The choice belongs to each of us.

Each seminar gave me the chance to try something different, to improve the approach, to experiment a little more. When I met with too much cynicism, it was difficult, but it confirmed my initial hypothesis. When I encountered intelligence and heart, it was magical. There was a method, yes, but mainly it was the quality of the participants that mattered.

As soon as one or two people decided to keep their mask and play little power games, it harmed the entire group. The effect was striking, and spoke volumes. Seeing it, how can anyone be surprised by the problems in our society?

Some people have trouble sharing. They want to shine at all cost. And all the time. A group can fall hostage to one ambitious and manipulative person if we let such a person take up too much room. **We are influenced by our surroundings.**

That's why it's important to refuse the unacceptable, because that forces everyone to behave better, with greater dignity. My seminars, like art therapy workshops, prove to what extent human beings can give their best when they are allowed to create in a context of trust and goodwill. Kindness and meanness are two sides of the same coin. It takes very little to push the coin over to one side or the other.

On a Saturday afternoon at the end of September, I was back in Montreal for a few days. A light fall breeze was blowing under a brilliant sun. I was strolling among the people on Sherbrooke Street.

By chance, we were in the midst of the International Festival of Films on Art, and I had every intention of taking advantage of it. I'd identified the films dealing with subjects that interested me. That afternoon at the Montreal Museum of Fine Arts, Jean-Pierre Krief's film, *Rage and Dreams of the Condemned,* had been like a gift to me.

"In the 1960s, Jimmy Boyle was the most wanted criminal in all of Scotland. Arrested and condemned to life imprisonment in 1967, he became the most dangerous inmate in Scottish prisons. Resisting a brutal and outmoded penitentiary system, he fought it inch by inch and stirred up violent revolts among the inmates wherever he was incarcerated. For six years he was enclosed naked in a cage, without any access to the outside world. Then one day he was invited to take part in a prison experiment, Barlinnie, founded on principles quite different from those of the traditional system. He discovered sculpture and was completely transformed. After twenty-six years behind bars, he was given parole. The film follows his extraordinary career and draws parallels with the climate prevailing in French prisons."[12]

The film shows how creative activity can break incarceration, and testifies to the importance of silence, freedom, confidence and experimentation. It confirmed my approach and my experiments during seminars, and encouraged me to continue in that direction. It was a sign. It was the answer for which I'd been waiting, and which I needed in order to go on.

A human being who seems to have started down the worst possible road might have a chance of turning off that road, if given the opportunity. That was the message I took from the film and which told me, in spite of all the obstacles and cynicism I sometimes encountered, that I mustn't abdicate. I had to continue the collective intelligence method: to foster the sharing of dreams, encourage freedom while respecting others, and promote belief in human values that unite us. Above all, everyone had to have the chance to create and contribute… to contribute just a little more dignity, humanity and pleasure.

THE ROAD OF DESIRES

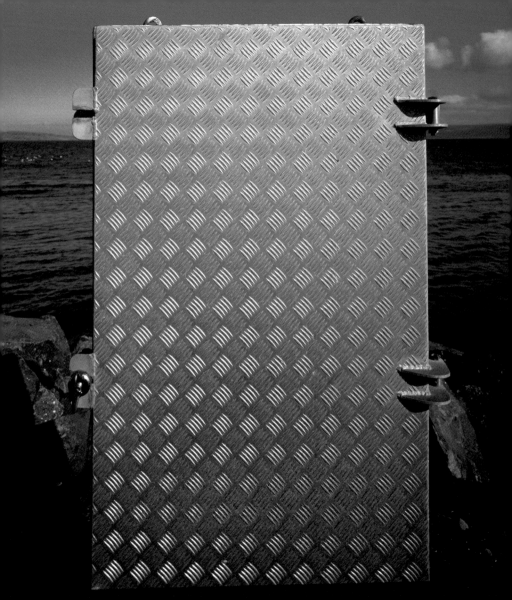

"You have to look for the line's desire, the point
at which it wants to come in or die…"

Matisse

3

The months of October and November had flown by. The proof: every page of my agenda was completely blackened whereas those of my journal were white, or almost.

On Sundays, in the midst of my whirlwind life, I would sometimes sit on a bench in Monceau Park, not far from my home, and think how the pace of my life had changed compared to that first year I'd lived in Paris.

My friend Marielle, her husband Jean, a painter, and their two boys lived next door. They had been among our first friends in Paris. My friendship with Marielle had probably played a decisive role in my decision to live there a while. By chance we'd found an apartment not far from them. I say chance because, in Paris, you don't have much choice. There's a permanent shortage of apartments. Any empty apartment is rented within twenty-four hours.

Sitting on that bench, I recalled the full year I'd lived there, returning only rarely to Montreal. It had rained a lot that year. The grey sky, conducive to dreaming, had led me into unexpected wandering. I was often alone with my imagination. I was distracted, rubbing shoulders with the imaginary as much as with reality, and sometimes barely distinguishing between them, as though the marvelous was taking possession of my reason.

I felt as though I was discovering a shadowy Paris, subtler than the City of Lights we first see. More poetic too, and more sober. It was as though I were in a strange and revealing fable. If only I'd realized sooner that the key to entering that world was those brief aimless moments of existence.

Until then, I'd always associated Paris with partying: nightly revelry, morning noise that lasted all day, and the contemporaneous murmur of dense crowds that makes one so impatient.

Then, one day, the slow walks had calmed my gaze, introducing shadows into the light. I had the feeling of seeing differently, maybe more with my heart than with my eyes.

I probably needed these brief pauses in my agitated life to make me let go, and see again. I had to acquire a degree of nonchalance to appreciate the real value of the chiaroscuro Paris light.

Atmospheric memories: like that summer evening in the courtyard of the Louvre at dusk. I can still hear my footsteps and those of my friend echo on the uneven paving stones. I see our silhouettes glide along in the bluish penumbra, projecting our shadows and secrets on the surrounding walls. We shared our desires and dreams there, as though naming them could give them life, make them come true.

In high antiquity, "man had the privilege of starting to name things, the breeze, cloud, grass, water..."[1] In our postmodern societies, we think everything has already been named, but our desires remain.

It's true that the road of desires does not reveal itself easily. Often we have to wander a while to discover it. It sometimes appears just when we've given up trying, out of desperation from looking for it too long, or simply out of a lack of time to create the empty space for it to enter. The road of desires winds through both the visible and invisible worlds. It's unattainable when we want to seize hold of it, and right there when we least expect it.

According to the ancient teachings of the Tao, "Desire and non-desire: these two spring from the same source. Only their names differ. They are Darkness and Mystery."[2]

Thus the road of desires is a mystery we try to pierce at particular moments in our life, probably those moments when we're most in touch with ourselves, most attentive. These moments are often dark and sad.

"But in truth it is in the furthest depths of this darkness that one may find the door. The door to the absolute, the marvellous,"[3] concludes the Tao.

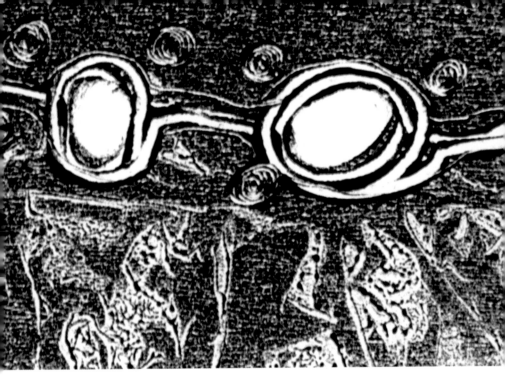

At times our desires become a beacon in the night, hope in the desert. They are so clear that they are almost palpable. They inhabit us completely. And once satisfied, forgotten or abandoned, they slip away almost unnoticed.

Like everything else, desires evolve or die. We must therefore take to the road from time to time to revive them. That was the goal of my wandering walks. To revive my desires. That was three years ago.

Since those days of wandering, I've thought of Paris as a strange labyrinth that fosters contemplation and beautiful solitude in the midst of crowds. Since then, I see shadowed plazas as so many hiding places for searching, perplexed minds, as mine was then.

Each experience, each encounter transforms us a little, and helps us become who we are. Knowing this, we are sometimes tempted to provoke them rather than await them. At least that's what happens to me, being so impatient. "When we wait violently for something, always, always, we have to be very balanced not to go mad and, in the end, find within ourselves the strength to cease waiting,"[4] writes Jean Giono. That was my situation exactly.

Take Paris, for example. I'd gone there a few times before, but in June 1999 an astonishing thing had happened.

As soon as I was free of my professional commitments, a little voice told me, "Why not live there?" The idea seemed ridiculous at first. Overloaded with obligations in North America, I couldn't imagine how that insidious little nonsensical phrase could have entered my head. But the moment I lay eyes on something beautiful, as soon as I let my guard down, that little voice would start tap-tap-tapping at my head again.

I realized that I'd never allowed myself such a folly. The very idea of stopping a while in a city rather than passing through it at top speed seemed like an unbelievable luxury! Of course, I'd thought about it. Often, in fact. But my responsibilities had always taken precedence over adventure.

Nor had fate ever intervened in that direction; from one obligation to the other, there had simply never been time.

Eventually, the great dreamer that I was had gradually lost the ability to dream.

But now, here was that desire resurfacing in such an unexpected manner, in all its evocative power. And along with the desire came a childish impatience, despite my forty-two well-seasoned years, to go through with this folly.

That's how, in less than a week, I decided to turn a crazy feeling into a crazy decision. I wanted Paris, its streets, its museums, its culture; more than that, I wanted to set reason aside and listen to that little voice, just to see how far it would take me.

I absolutely did not want to analyze my decision, fearing that my reason would send me along the path of more calculated risks. The last thing I wanted was to calculate anything.

But the fascinating city of Paris was not what prompted my first desire. What really prompted it was an intuition of fortuitous encounters to come, which would lead me to better understand the world and its humanist possibilities.

Like the poet Christian Bobin, "I expect something from everyone I meet and, because I expect it, I get it."[5]

That was the state I was in when I chose Paris. Whenever my reason tried to shake my resolve, I'd think of Gérard Macé's words in his memoirs about reading, *Gossip Mongering*[1]:

"'What we can't reach by flying, we must reach by limping': this warning by Rückert, or long-forgotten advice, reminds me that falling is not so far from taking flight, to the point where falling is the human, awkward form of flying. It also reminds me that, thanks to our dormant vigilance, a sudden lucky accident can pull us out of the hole where we had unwittingly buried ourselves: the slightest break in our habits awakens old desires and a momentary inattention on the uneven pavement can sometimes allow us to regain our memory."[6]

To regain my memory; that's what I really wanted. It was as though, to really take flight, I had to risk falling. It was something I'd always known, but this time the unknown was far greater. For the first time, I wasn't sure what I was looking for. I had no precise goal, only a desire: to enchant my life.

The unknown is attractive because it carries the promise of new learning. I like the first steps, that time when the unknown is not yet familiar, when we catch glimpses of the marvelous.

It reminds me of the excitement I felt each autumn on going back to school. Not because of school: I was attracted to the fountain pens, the pencils and brand new notebooks in which I made such an effort at first. It was the atmosphere of new books, the smell of paper and ink that excited me. I was drunk on the idea of discovering new worlds through them. I loved the evenings I spent alone, sitting at my desk in my room.

I longed for autumn. Its fresh air and winds brought back the desire to study and awakened my senses and imagination. Even today, for me, autumn is a season of joy, and I sometimes feel nostalgic for those first days back at school. In fact, going to live in Paris gave me the feeling of starting a new school year.

The first lesson my French friends taught me was the art of living. I should say "my European friends" because, among my friends in France, there are as many Italians, Belgians, Swiss, English, Germans... which is what makes the circle so enriching.

Each meal taken together became a pretext to remake the world. My inclinations were well nourished. I felt twenty years younger, reliving those fervent nights when we put everything into question to sketch out a new world, rocked by the era and words of John Lennon: "You may say I'm a dreamer, but I'm not the only one."

That was the atmosphere my French friends created for me. I'm telling you all this because I'd begun this book in a completely different tone. I wanted to sketch the qualities of the new leaders of the third millennium, and attempt a modest forecast of management trends, while proposing some ideas for a better future.

But it seemed to me that we've so segmented life that we now look on companies and their artisans as though they lived on another planet. Unless you offer recipes for accelerating performance to boost quarterly profits for shareholders, you can forget it. No one listens, unless you couch your words in the specialized technical or financial jargon that pleases market analysts.

What's more, it's no longer necessary to even make a pretense of regret when announcing bad news. Try it: announce four hundred layoffs and you'll see company share values shoot up.

I'm not against reductions in personnel; I believe a company must continue to perform and renew itself constantly. It's a basic characteristic of any living organism. But, it seems to me, such an organism should live as much for the development of its potential, and that of its collaborators and clients, as to enrich its shareholders in the short term. I see an imbalance in current trends. Many decisions are made with an eye only to shareholders. If such is the case, I don't see the need for managers. We could let shareholders run companies. We'd save on salaries!

Does a company have to perform for its shareholders and cut thousands of jobs in a single day? When a business renews itself regularly, it has no need to cut a thousand jobs at a time because it has the courage, every year, to put itself in question in order to continue its development.

Furthermore, someone who finds fulfillment in their work and continues to develop has no trouble finding a job (if they lose theirs). It's an opportunity for different experiences. The problem occurs when hundreds of people are let go on the same day in the same city.

A "responsible" business encourages the development of its personnel. This doesn't mean it should adopt a paternalistic management style; it is an insult to human beings to turn adults into children. I don't believe that employees should ever let anyone make them abdicate their responsibility to themselves. Our destiny belongs to us alone.

I prefer companies and unions to be concerned with the evolution of their personnel, their community and society as a whole, while maintaining some distance. It's a question of elegance and respect, an attitude that can best be described by the simple word "care."

This means caring about the effects of our acts, thinking a little bit about the human, community and social impact of our decisions. It comes back again to the much discussed and so rarely practiced word "ethics."

More and more people are opting for equitable products. Some of us have decided to act. We are finally beginning to understand our power. Isn't it time employees also began to concern themselves with their company? People shouldn't wait for their employer to do everything. They should think about what they can contribute in exchange. It's a question of reciprocity and co-evolution. We're all partly responsible for the context of our lives. Companies are what we make of them. Those who think of themselves as victims of a system actively participate in reinforcing the oppressive aspects of that system.

The danger is that we become little tin soldiers, docile and executing orders, letting our lives pass without living them, and no longer letting our desires, ideas and solidarity emerge in our work. Many people have a life and a job, as though the two could be dissociated, stuck in two separate compartments. As though our left and right brains did not communicate. As though emotion could be controlled by a switch we simply flip on and off when we choose.

The human being is such a complex organism that it has been broken into segments, supposedly to help us progress more rapidly. But we do not stop being whole persons because we work for a business or institution. It seems to me that, after having split everything up, we're ready for a grand reintegration. Modernity, with its compartments, separations, disciplines and expert jargons, would have little use for the talents of a man like Leonardo da Vinci.

I sometimes imagine the human treasure that lies entombed in companies, buried under bureaucratic job descriptions.

We shrug off these little daily deaths, thinking them banal and innocuous. In the economic war that assails us, my concerns are those of Saint-Exupéry: "What torments me can't be cured by soup kitchens. What torments me are not these pockmarks, those bumps, or this ugliness. It's how, in each of these men, a little of Mozart is assassinated."[7]

As time passes, I find business messages more and more boring. I look for some depth and knowledge, but often find the opposite. I look for something to encourage accomplishment and evolution, but I often find no more than an ambition for accounting. I worry that we are silent and docile in the face of such sterile discourses that reduce the world to finances. The people with whom I spent my evenings in Paris lived outside corporate walls, and I began feeling that I needed to step out of that frame. My friends made me want to play hooky. And in this spirit of freedom, I learned the most of all.

"The devil is boredom," writes director Peter Brook, speaking of the theatre. What would he say about schools, companies, institutions? Would he find them boring? It seems to me that his thought should inspire us to reform the various theatres of our learning, that is, our schools and companies. The quality of the space around us influences the quality of our relationships. In the theatre, people work in a space of proximity and learn to see one another, and this contributes to the transformation of each person who participates. Isn't the same true in organizations and in society?

Our spaces are so encumbered with prejudices and predefined practices that we no longer see each other. Our mirrors are fogged up. "... For something of quality to happen," explains Peter Brook, "an empty space must first be created. An empty space allows a new phenomenon to emerge. If you look carefully at every aspect of spectacle, at everything concerning content, meaning, even expression, speech, music, gestures, relationships, impact, the memory we can keep within ourselves... all this exists only if the possibility of a fresh new experience also exists. But no fresh new experience is possible without there being first a naked, virgin, pure space to receive it."[8]

This is why companies that are too rigid unknowingly impede the creativity of those working in them. They fill up all the space and every instant so that managing the oversupply of information, methods, techniques and numbers takes up all the time that could have been used for collective thinking, creation and achievement. Instead, teams are trained to be managers of the useless, and weary followers.

Just as we must rid ourselves of our old clothes to make room for the new, without emptiness, we block the emergence of new things.

Locked in our certainties and bureaucracies, it's difficult to foster evolution and creativity.

Taylor, the scientist who invented a method to organize factory work by maximizing the use of tools and eliminating useless movement, could not have imagined, even in his wildest dreams, that we would apply his theory to the management of knowledge. In this, the students have surpassed their teacher.

To listen to some consultants describe Knowledge Management, you'd think they were describing a flawless and predictable mechanism. It's stupefying that they could think such a mechanism would awaken intelligence and help to manage knowledge.

It seems that we now invent names arbitrarily, as if accuracy of meaning were no longer important. As if the objective were to find catchy words to sell methods that simulate improved performance and make the tin soldiers more profitable.

We no longer have time to rethink our methods of working. We look for the quick formula that requires the least thought and impresses shareholders. What's important is to know how to sell it so as to make it profitable as fast as possible.

But all this is smoke and mirrors. The kind of people we are will influence the kind of organizations we build. There's a close link between the two. We can't go on for very long being moronic at work and intelligent at home. The social cost of such attitudes is likely to be very high. **We are influenced by our surroundings.** Yet, above all, we shouldn't admit defeat too quickly, because awakening our desires gives meaning to our lives and fosters the development of strengths and talents to achieve our desires. The resulting passion propels our effort. We can't accomplish anything collectively if we don't begin by giving ourselves as individuals permission to experience life fully, to be present in the world.

The 20th century was the era of specialists. To head a business, senior managers are often obliged to be well versed in process engineering or finance. Despite the fine speeches, the development of human beings is often low down on the organizational list of priorities. We want specialists and technicians when we need generalists with multiple talents, multiple curiosities. We especially need more openness. But, during the last two centuries, we've mostly learned to create models and apply procedures and methods that are supposedly proven to work. Doesn't the job, for example, of a human resources specialist (this title already puts men and women down on the same level as financial, technical or material resources) resemble the application of accounting techniques more than the development of people and teams? Although managers ought to be accompanying their team, listening, stimulating and encouraging, they rarely have time to do so. They're too busy going through hundreds of emails, returning phone calls, managing the collective bargaining agreement and setting up meetings.

It's revealing to stand back and look at oneself. If, trapped in this economic cogwheel, we could stand back just a few steps and look behind us, what would we see? Isn't the absolute economy becoming Law in every facet of our lives, including the most intimate ones? It's as though the old dream in *The Book of Prince Shang* was coming true, or almost. The authors of that book lived in the 5th and 4th century B.C., before China became an empire. "No other text of political theory ever written, from Machiavelli to Lenin, expresses so horrifically the dream of an absolutism that annihilates every other way of thinking, every other feeling or human desire, building the terrifying edifice of the Law and Force," explains Pietro Citati. "The authors of that text had all the qualities to accomplish their dream: formidably logical minds, an abstract contempt for human beings, inexorable cruelty, a hatred of all compromise, a will that retreats before no obstacle, a desperate solitude and the inability to think of and love the world as a constantly moving play of contradictions."[9]

We may not yet be there, but are we that far away?

We have volunteered, unconsciously, for the same war: the war of numbers. How long will we remain entranced before the mantra of "Think Big," where nothing is ever big enough to satisfy us?

Mega-companies are more and more numerous. This collective megalomania extends into every field. We are obsessed with excess. "Uniqueness is no longer defined by its meaning but by its format. If you succeed in attracting a thousand, or a million pairs of eyes, rather than one or a few, you've won a place in history,"[10] writes journalist Jean-Pierre Denis. Everything is a question of quantity. And uniformity.

Twenty years ago, driving from one American city to another, I was horrified to find the same chain stores everywhere, the same colors, the same storefronts.

The cities all looked so alike, it was as though my car wasn't moving. Today the same thing is happening in my own country. Meanwhile, big-box stores are strangling neighboring small businesses. More and more we are opting for mega.

This trend is transforming the global scene. At this point, if we move a pawn, the whole chessboard moves. Because the game is global, it affects more players.

When a chain of stores is sold or shut down it has a negative impact on thousands of people in several countries at once. This complicates any analysis of the consequences of our acts. Contradictions increase the complexity of the game and its systems. And we're playing faster all the time, with less and less time to think.

Since the beginning of time, what have human beings always needed to fulfill themselves, if not to love, learn, create, endeavor and understand? Have we really changed? I don't think so.

Time seems to be what's missing. If our desires are in retreat, it's not for want of trying to satisfy them as quickly as possible. Our lifespan grows longer, but our space-time, encumbered with a thousand and one occupations and agitations, is rapidly shrinking.

We live in a constant state of urgency. "It's no longer a question of trying to master time," Zaki Laïdi reminds us in *The Tyranny of Urgency,* "but rather of trying to avoid being "out of time" like a runner completely bypassed by the pace of the race."[11]

We need the eye and camera of Wim Wenders to follow us, step by step, and preserve the traces of our drifting, emotional or otherwise. Our lives are becoming road movies.

All this makes me want to suspend time. I imagine a remote control that would allow me to put the world on pause for a few hours, while I go about my tasks. Then, when I set the world in motion again, I would get the most out of it, thanks to the free time I would have gained.

We're all the same. We'd like to stop time when it suits us. Time, we're told, will be the most valuable commodity in the third millennium. The true challenge of our overactive lives is to protect, against all odds, some free time for our desires.

In François Cheng's magnificent novel, *The Story of Tianyi,* there's a beautiful passage on desire: "Reading Rimbaud, I remember my thoughts in the Sichuan valleys: if Man is an animal who's always thirsty, then nature, provider of water, is able to quench his desire. It must be that creation engenders no desires that it cannot satisfy. In short, Man is thirsty because water exists. Man, yes, is free to desire, but he can only desire what unfathomable reality already contains. Even when he goes so far as to desire the infinite, it's only because the infinite is already there waiting for him. Everything happens as though whatever we desire most were already contained within that desire; otherwise, how could we have desired it?"[12]

I too believe that the satisfaction of desire can be found in desire itself, and that any subordination that keeps us apart from ourselves puts our life at risk. For several years already, I'd thought about my desires and about the importance of encouraging others to desire.

For the sake of my desires, three years earlier, I'd turned my life upside down. And I got to like it: the proof is that I'm about to do it again in a few months.

I'd created real disorder back then, which at times perplexed those around me. I wanted to reach to the depths of myself. I was searching, fumbling for a meaning and I think, like François Cheng's protagonist, that, "if it is my destiny on earth to wander, at least I can transform it into an impassioned quest whose goal would one day be revealed to me."[13] I too am of that same mettle. I need a quest and passion. I accept my nature and all the good and bad that stems from it.

As for my thoughts on the importance of encouraging others to desire, I owe them to my readers. Some of their correspondence was overwhelming. Some writers announced, with passion and enthusiasm, that they'd quit their job or changed their life completely after reading *City of Intelligences*. I grew afraid that my writing on dream and desire, on the need to overcome our fears and embrace life passionately, would have greater impact than I'd wanted.

At the time, I'd wanted to share my convictions. I was a bit fed up with the predominant pessimism and the spirit of victimization that I all too often came up against. I felt like saying, and still do: it's not too late, we can still make a difference. Let's wake up.

Wings of desire

This said, who am I to tell others what to do? I don't know any more than you do what a person has to do to be happy. I don't have the formula for happiness, nor the one to make the world a better place. That's why this book is more like a journal and reflections than an essay. I wanted to share my flaws and doubts so that you might better judge my opinions and convictions.

I only hope that those who made major decisions after reading *City* will not regret their choices. The winding road is often harder, but I think it is the most satisfying. In any case, can a book trigger something in us that isn't already there? I don't think so. I see it more as revealing a desire that was already waiting for its moment to emerge.

"This conditioned freedom of human desire," François Cheng says, "far from abasing or limiting human existence, lifts it up and enlarges it. It places it at the heart of a vast mystery. And makes the human adventure less unreal."[14]

To open wide the doors of desires and give more meaning to our life. To dare to fly without knowing exactly where we'll land. It's a beautiful risk that cuts through the monotony of a life that's merely slotted in the corridor of our certi

But from where will our desires be born. Where shall we in a our sources of enlightenment?

Already in his day, Goethe wrote, "Men are so inclined to content themselves with what is commonest; the spirit and the senses so easily grow dead to the impressions of the beautiful and perfect, that every one should study, by all methods, to nourish in his mind the faculty of feeling these things. For no man can bear to be entirely deprived of such enjoyments: it is only because they are not used to taste of what is excellent, that the generality of people take delight in silly and insipid things, provided they be new. For this reason... one ought every day at least to hear a little song, read a good poem, see a fine picture, and, if it were possible, to speak a few reasonable words."[15]

What we are is part of what shapes our society. We create other human beings in our image and nourish them with the same things with which we nourish ourselves. A sensibility develops, sometimes slowly over time, sometimes in dazzling leaps. That's why we have to implore artists and poets to live close to us, to help us see Beauty, which escapes us far too often, and to share their utopias with us.

I wanted more and more freedom in my seminars, and I pushed the experiments a little further each time. My clients' trust in me allowed me to employ an increasingly artistic approach, and it produced marvels.

The positive returns were not long in coming. My clients seemed absolutely thrilled. I was touched by their many comments. Brigitte's, for example: "A beautiful demonstration through experimentation of the power of collective creation… and of building in successive layers, just as geological strata form mountains." Or this message from Marielle: "The seminar was a great experience for me; I've never witnessed a reversal of such magnitude."

It was a fine way to end, because I'd decided, after several years of collaboration, that it was time to let them fly on their own. It was up to them to take their destiny in hand.

If the learning chain is working, the departure of a consultant goes unnoticed. Without autonomy, the collective intelligence process fails.

A consultant can in no way substitute for the managers in place. To know how and when to leave is as important as a successful entrance.

We'd proven that we could have fun while thinking about and discussing very serious issues. The most oft repeated comment was: "Thank you for those intense moments of enjoyment; they really gave me a second wind."

To awaken desire… that's all I want from now on. I once sought to change the world. But as I grew older I realized it was impossible. Now I'm trying to follow the advice of Francis of Assisi. As soon as I stand still, my desires go quiet, and my source dries up, I change worlds.

Still seated on my bench in Monceau Park, I realized how true François Cheng's remarks on desire really were. When I'd chosen Paris, three years earlier, I knew almost no one there and I had no contracts.

Once I'd rented an apartment on a whim and the first monthly bills started coming in, I got a shiver of fright. I had to ask myself if I was crazy. It was a leap into the void, the unknown... Nor did I have the financial means to absorb a failure. Our Parisian endeavor was a risky move for our company, very risky, in fact.

The little voice I'd heeded had been so subtle, I had to wonder if I'd heard it right. I was afraid I might even have invented it. And yet, several months later, a French publisher had accepted my book and I had contracts that would allow me to live and work in the enchanting city that is Paris.

It was another dream come true, and one more proof that we can broaden our life by desiring. It was a sign, too, that encouraged me to keep taking risks based on my intuition. It was one more proof that "everything happens as though whatever we desire most were already contained within that desire."

I fastened the collar of my coat. The leaves on the old trees shook gently in the cool breeze. Everything seemed so beautiful that morning in the park, which was bathed in a soft autumn light. I abandoned the bench to continue my walk. The paths stretched nonchalantly in front of me amid the tumble of cascading leaves.

I recalled reading, somewhere, that wonderful things come to those who are filled with wonder. That morning, I had to agree.

Paris, October-November 2002

DREAMWEAVERS

"As long as people can escape to the realm of fairy tales, they are full of nobility, compassion and poetry. In the realm of everyday life they are, alas, more prone to caution, mistrust and suspicion."[1]

Milan Kundera

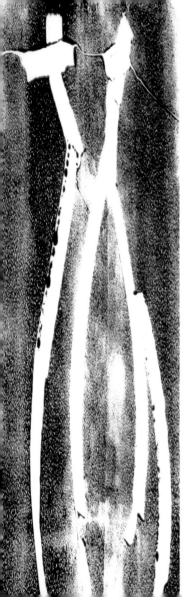

4

I returned to Quebec for a few days. It was cold. That year, winter had come early. There had been snow on the ground since November. It was shaping up to be a long winter, which I was happy to interrupt with occasional trips to Paris.

I was giving a conference in the beautiful Manicouagan region of northern Quebec. I'd fallen in love with the landscape there. During the conference, I noticed a tiny flame in their eyes; the desire to reinvent was blazing there. I was scheduled to go back and do additional work with them in January, and was looking forward to the experience.

Back in Paris, my first night was sleepless. My body seemed to have overdosed on successive jetlags. During my night of insomnia, I read a short book by Eric-Emmanuel Schmitt entitled *Monsieur Ibrahim and the Flowers of the Koran*.

I noted the following excerpt in my journal:

"Monsieur Ibrahim, when I say that smiling is for the rich, I mean it's something for people who are happy."

"Well, that's where you're wrong. Smiling is what makes you happy."

The next day, my fatigue played tricks on me. I got up without much enthusiasm, but with a smile just the same. I was happy to be back in Paris for several weeks.

As soon as I stepped outside, I noticed there were crowds everywhere, in the streets, the stores. The slightest errand became an expedition. It was early December and already the atmosphere of Christmas and shopping had taken over the city.

In the tearoom where I stopped for a bite to eat, three young women shoved their way in front of me rudely, like urchins, although they were well into their thirties. I looked them in the eye, thinking it might embarrass them. Not in the least. I thought, courtesy is disappearing, even in the better neighborhoods of Paris.

Having finally finished my shopping, I was almost home when I took a bad fall on rue Boissy d'Anglade, and sprained my ankle.

No wonder: my arms were full of packages and my head was in the clouds. I was captivated by the beautiful sky that evening, the immense moon from time to time breaking through the large clouds sailing by.

In what followed, I was very disappointed by people's attitudes. I'd fallen beside a large hotel, the Crillon. Nearby, a security guard manned a barricade outside the American embassy. He didn't move a muscle to help me. Among the passersby, someone was grumbling over the high price of a Christmas Eve meal at the Crillon. They watched me get to my feet without raising a finger. A man who'd seen me from a distance, stopped when he reached me: "You're all right?" Thank you, I am. By then I was already back on my feet.

I took a moment to look around me, just to be sure that I'd really seen all these people looking at me without the slightest compassion. It was as though I was a virtual character to them. They watched me fall without moving.

It reminded me of Ernesto Sabato's discussion of insensitivity in *Resistance*. I was young and in good shape; my fall wasn't serious. But if I'd been old and weak, I doubt that it would have made any difference.

Are we anesthetized to the point where we're indifferent to the misfortune of others? Such indifference had shocked and saddened me. My fatigue was certainly partly responsible, but I had the fleeting selfish thought that I was going to a lot of trouble for people who, in the end, couldn't care less about others. We were a long way from the spirit of the maxim: Liberty, Equality, Fraternity. Luckily I found a cab right away and, in the space of five minutes, the driver, a very nice young man, made me forget the indifference I had encountered earlier.

The sprain turned out to be worse than I'd thought at first, and I found myself immobilized at home for several days. My foot was swollen and turning black. I'd torn a ligament. I smiled at the vicissitudes of life. Despite being utterly worn out for some time, I'd stubbornly kept on working. Now life had taken charge of slowing me down.

Stuck at home without much food, and unwilling to bother the guard downstairs or my friends, I imagined what it would be like to be an elderly woman alone in the world. I felt even more compassion for those people we forget too often, and even more concern for this world that seemed to be losing all sense of solidarity.

I took advantage of this period of inactivity, and of the long silences, to reenergize myself, and finish reading the autobiography of Pablo Neruda, a committed man who remained compassionate throughout his life. I wondered how we might initiate a movement towards a new solidarity. How could we imitate Garcia Lorca who, according to Neruda, knew how to multiply beauty? "Happiness," Neruda wrote, "was in his skin."

I managed to hold my last meetings and complete the work I'd already started. At last it was time for a vacation. My sweetheart would join me in Paris.

Because of my ankle, our planned trip to the south of Spain, where we were going to stay in an old Moorish palace in the midst of sumptuous countryside, was no longer possible. We might manage a few days in Rome if my ankle healed. Otherwise, we'd stay in Paris.

It was fabulous to be able to live in two cities, two countries, two continents.
I dreamed of eventually adding a third.

Living in a new city changes the perspective of your gaze;
it gives you the time to develop quiet habits,
to slowly discover the images and symbols of a place,
and the rituals of its inhabitants.

We are lucky to live in a society of images. A dream, a concept, a fantasy, an idea can be rapidly shared with millions of people. We have the opportunity to feed our imaginations more rapidly than ever. The possibilities of metaphors abound, but it's as though we're fixated on violence, sex and money.

The great Brazilian photographer Sebastião Salgado, who travels the world and spends much of his time among victims of famine, war and poverty, states: "For a long time, we sought to make Esperanto the international language. In the end, I believe the international language is the image! What we write in images in the Ivory Coast can be read in Japan, China or Brazil without requiring translation."[2]

The image ought to bring us closer to each other, and allow us to better communicate with each other. Unfortunately, it's not yet the case.

It's as though we prefer the image that kills to the one that unites.

"I used to think that humanity was evolving positively, toward progress. I realized that we can also go in the other direction, and that real human intelligence is our ability to adapt. Humans get used to anything, including the worst. In Bosnia, children set off every day for school under the bombardments, almost the same way my son goes to school every morning," the photographer adds.

"They had adapted to war. In Rwanda, I saw a father throw his dead child on a pile of 10,000 corpses, then go off and drink a tea, as though nothing had happened. He too had adapted. That's what's so overwhelming: the incredible capacity of human beings to survive, but also to destroy. Sometimes I wonder if we have the right combination of genes, if our real nature isn't individualism and violence."[3]

Sebastião Salgado ends with this question: "Can we really continue this mad race forward while abandoning the majority of humanity? Can we reconcile the planet of humans?"[4]

We have powerful means at our disposal, yet we've never been so powerless. The image, for example, is incredibly powerful and technology allows us to broadcast it instantly throughout the world. It ought to shock us, mobilize us, make us act, but it ends up inuring us to the worst. We adapt to the atrocities of humanity.

One of the big questions I've been asking myself for some time now is why violence is increasingly becoming our favorite entertainment. I was worrying about it twenty years ago, and I see that the trend has continued to grow. It perplexes me. I'm often told that young people can tell the difference between movies, games and real life. Perhaps. If they live in a balanced home environment (and even then, I wonder). I still have a feeling (or conviction) that the images in our unconscious play a role in the construction of reality.

Sociologist Michel Maffesoli believes that such images awaken in us the desire to live with intensity. "A bandit without fear of death who risks his life is asleep in each of us. We can live it vicariously but, even as fantasy, it expresses our need for darkness, our desire for the 'accursed share' that modernity thought it had finally eliminated for good."[5] So much for the accursed share, but some of us may not be content to live vicariously. Couldn't this desire be an impulse (or simply a good idea) to act rather than fantasize? I can't help but see the connection. Imitation, it seems to me, is the most natural form of unconscious learning that there is. We do as the other person does, without even realizing it. If, in addition, imitation will make heroes of us, why would we hesitate before taking action in reality?

Thinking this, I wonder if we underestimate the symbolic power of images and their effect on our behavior. Isn't there a connection between the content of some entertainment products and this form of learning that comes to us so naturally, to "do as others do," with this "other" being someone we saw last night on TV or in a movie? Does reality go beyond fiction? Or does fiction feed reality?

I sometimes wish I had wings to fly high enough to see phenomena from above. I'd like to rise to a meta-level. I'd like someone to help me make the connections between the parts so as to better understand the whole. It may be complicated, but I'd still like to understand the causes and influences.

I'd like to slip behind things and events. I'd like to sneak behind the curtain, to become a shadow, so as to gain a little more understanding.

In fact, I'm afraid that, once again, we're adapting, and minimizing the increasing violence in the world. One thing's for sure, we all have the potential for violence within us. That much we can no longer deny.

"The first intelligent species on earth, we've placed our abilities in the service of the devil. We kill other species, massacre each other, multiply at an abnormal rate and waste the world's resources; the poor get poorer while the rich get richer, and that's just for starters," writes anthropologist Serge Bouchard in his column in the Montreal daily *Le Devoir*.[6]

We take in these observations with our breakfast, our first sip of coffee. They ought to make us think, unsettle us for at least part of the day. They rarely do. Something else quickly distracts us. For the more sensitive among us, it becomes a daily effort not to descend into pessimism. We shut ourselves in our own bubbles to go on living happily. I hope that, as the first intelligent species, now working to produce artificial intelligence, we will take time to think and to make the connections to understand better, before we start copying things exactly as they are.

What good is our fabulous intelligence if it is used to produce so much cruelty? Perhaps the poet Gilles Vigneault has the answer: "Freed of the barbarity of instinct, intelligence will only produce more barbarity."[7] It does not bode well. But if we reintegrated emotion with reason, if we allowed life to express itself freely with the ordinary disorder of the living, we might rediscover a little of that instinct.

We seem to be shutting ourselves in a bubble. I wonder if our slumber could one day be interrupted.

We ought to compose a symphony to life, rather than an early requiem.

I want to believe it's not too late. But to succeed, we must reach everyone, especially those who think they're not concerned. We form a whole, and one of our mistakes has surely been to confine ourselves in the shelter of our specializations.

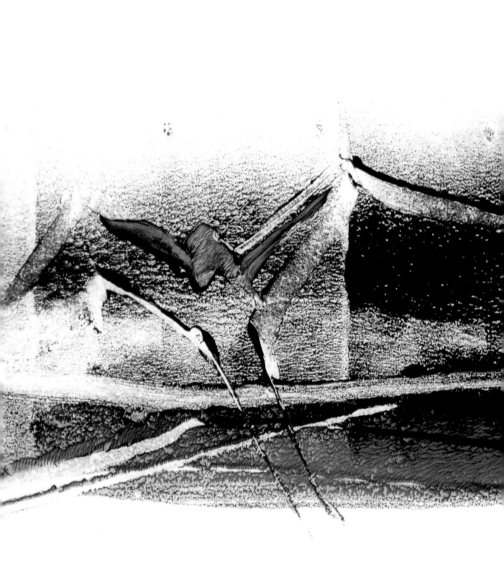

We think it's enough to use wizardry with numbers, with accounting, to improve people's performance.

Organizations would be surprised by the results if they were to change tactics and try instead to nourish the imagination of their people by encouraging them to develop personally and collectively.

This is one example where the parts could advance the cause of the whole. It's incredible how much organizations could do to contribute to the evolution of a new society.

But denunciations and writing are not enough. Many of us can exchange ideas, but the important thing is that some have the courage to act and to accept the attendant risks. "Very few people are capable of both ideas and action," declares the hero of Goethe's *Wilhelm Meister's Apprenticeship*. "Ideas enlarge, but they paralyze; action vivifies but restrains."[8]

To encourage thought and action to join forces, I'd like meetings to resemble the nights of my adolescence. I would lay a carpet down on the floor. Its contours would be our guideposts. From it, we would dream how to stage the marvelous and weave it into the organization's strategic plan, leaving the actors enough freedom to feel, see and interpret it so they can make it theirs. Planning is nothing more than exploring the future. To see into the distance, we must first believe it's possible.

Some find my ideas abstract. They would prefer an analytical grid that they could apply immediately. I want to give them blank pages and then look at what surprises their imagination has in store for them.

I want them to create disorder because, like Goethe, I believe that "people accomplish the extraordinary on the fringes of order."[10]

I dream we could be many to accomplish the extraordinary. That may be my utopia. I know that people often find my ideas unreasonable, but I console myself knowing I'm not the only one to wish the extraordinary could happen. I've heard from enough people on that score to confirm this. And then, "We won't be too hard on reason," Goethe continues, "and we'll recognize that the extraordinary is almost always beyond reason."[10]

I dream of women and men who will enchant the world, including those organizations who think that profits alone enchant. Yet, it's the opposite that is taking place; the world is becoming disenchanted. Let me be clear: I'm not against profits. I'm simply saying that they can't always be central. In fact, profits are marvelous if they help us live better together, help us share and find happiness along the way. Isn't the road we travel as important as our destination?

I say yes to profit, but not at any price. If life is sacrificed for profit, it raises serious questions for me. I'm always astonished by the anguished look of people who possess billions. They'll arrive at their destination frustrated, having accumulated rather than enjoyed. When the majority of people lack the basics, can those who have everything really be happy

The riches of the world will belong to fewer and fewer people. Can we reverse this trend? I write this with a great deal of hope, but very little expectation.

The figures cited by Jacques Attali are terrifying: "The average income in the richest countries was three times higher than in the poorest in 1820. It rose to 11 times higher in 1913, to 35 times higher in 1950, 44 times higher in 1973, 72 times higher in 1993. The richest 20% of humanity receives 86% of world revenues, compared to only 1% for the poorest 20%. The total wealth of the poorest billion human beings is actually equal to that of the one hundred richest!"[11]

I'm familiar with this trend, and it's no cause for celebration. I'd like to think we can still reverse it, that it's not too late to act.

I'd like us to become more connected. I have the feeling that we've been reduced to this situation because we've become detached from each other.

We think it's none of our business. We leave it to the legal profession, to politicians and police to decide. We criticize what doesn't work, thinking it justifies our retreating into ourselves.

If we don't wake up soon, we'll find ourselves living in protected enclaves, afraid of the rest of the world. If we don't react, our only contact with others who are different from us will be through virtual images.

We must create a chain, a chain in which each link helps the others to help others. A chain of small and grand gestures. A chain in which each of us is an important link whatever our role in society. A chain in which the loss of a single link robs the whole of its beauty. A goldsmith's masterpiece woven with the filigree of each one of our hearts.

The key to achieving this could perhaps be to learn to retell our dreams to weave modern tales, thereby helping us, as Kundera might say, be more compassionate, more noble and more poetic.

In my seminars, I get participants to dream, and then encourage them to compose stories based on their reverie. It's a step that brings people closer together and inevitably provides pleasure. Sharing our dreams requires that we make others see a concept by projecting it into an invented future.

It's wonderful and effective to share the experience of a dream. In the words of Matisse: "For me, the sensation comes first, then the idea." Dreams and desires are also sensations before they're ideas. Explaining them would be less effective than making them live. The only way to make them live, with emotion, is to present them in the form of tales, to weave them into stories.

What's more, the creation of stories requires that we find metaphors that yield understanding and meaning. Similarly, we find the thread of coherence in our nightly dreams by describing them when we awaken, to try to understand them.

"Past images reawakened in dreams are immediate, intense and without logical sequence," explains neuroscientist G. Lakoff. "This past that resurfaces takes the form of metaphor, because metaphor is a kind of analogical thinking that we use every day: we have little use for metaphors when we're engaged in precision activities or a clear thought, but when we're uncertain or don't understand what's going on, when confusion dulls our consciousness, metaphors help us to think."[12]

The more we talk about a desire, the more it takes shape in our being. The more we help others to see our reveries, the more, unconsciously, we find the key to achieving them.

The story here becomes a form of knowledge, linking desires, facts people and things. What makes this approach even more interesting is when the work is done collectively. All the individual slices of dream come together to form one big collective dream. Then we have to call on theatrical methods to present it, because the big challenge is to allow others to experience it so that the chain of the dream extends to all who hear it.

"Sheherazade's great art, through which she saves herself every night, consists in knowing how to link stories together and when to interrupt them: two operations relating to continuity and discontinuity of time. The secret is in the rhythm, in a way of capturing time that seems to date back to the ancient times: in the meter of epic verse, in the various means of sustaining the desire to hear what comes next in prose narrative," Calvino explains.[13] To enable the other to see, but also to create desire, to awaken the desire to create and to live what follows. It's up to us to enrich our present by anticipating the future.

In his confessions, Saint Augustine reflects similarly: "For if there are times past and future, I wish to know where they are. But if I have not yet succeeded in this, I still know that wherever they are, they are not there as future or past, but as present. For if they are there as future, they are there as "not yet"; if they are there as past, they are there as "no longer." Wherever they are and whatever they are they exist therefore only as present. Although we tell of past things as true, they are drawn out of the memory — not the things themselves, which have already passed, but words constructed from the images of the perceptions which were formed in the mind, like footprints in their passage through the senses. My childhood, for instance, which is no longer, still exists in time past, which does not now exist. But when I call to mind its image and speak of it, I see it in the present because it is still in my memory.

"Whether there is a similar explanation for the foretelling of future events — that is, of the images of things which are not yet seen as if they were already existing — I confess, O my God, I do not know. But this I certainly do know: that we generally think ahead about our future actions, and this premeditation is in time present; but that the action which we premeditate is not yet, because it is still future. When we shall have started the action and have begun to do what we were premeditating, then that action will be in time present, because then it is no longer in time future.

"Whatever may be the manner of this secret foreseeing of future things, nothing can be seen except what exists. But what exists now is not future, but present. When, therefore, they say that future events are seen, it is not the events themselves, for they do not exist as yet (that is, they are still in time future), but perhaps, instead, their causes and their signs are seen, which already do exist. Therefore, to those already beholding these causes and signs, they are not future, but present, and from them future things are predicted because they are conceived in the mind. These conceptions, however, exist now, and those who predict those things see these conceptions before them in time present."[14]

I think we could make progress on the human front if we were more conscious of this great power of ours. My collective intelligence approach is really nothing more than these few steps of a natural process of anticipation and creation.

First, let's imagine a better world by dreaming it and desiring it together. Then, let's give our collective dream some life with the aid of many metaphors, by inventing modern stories. Then pass it on to as many people as possible. Then we'll see what effect it has on real creations. When those first creations appear, let's preserve their traces to revive our collective memory and continue to project ourselves into the future. It's an invitation to stage beauty and to carefully conserve its traces, to sow our future dreams, as a reminder to keep our dreams alive.

This is my dream and my belief. We build our own lives just as we build the society in which we live.

Without lapsing into superstition or into those rituals that just appease us in times of doubt, the latest scientific discoveries demonstrate that our brain needs to create myths and to express them in rituals to function optimally.[15] The ritual I propose is the creation of stories.

For Joseph Campbell, myths help us settle our existential fears. We need to find a balance, despite all the mystery around us. Life. Death. Our place in the universe. Natural disasters. The violence of humans along with their goodness. Myths, with the help of metaphors, let us reconcile opposites.

In the book *Why God Won't Go Away*, fifteen researchers studied the brain's actions during periods of meditation and spiritual activity. They noted that neurobiological processes allow human beings to transcend material existence and connect to a deeper, more spiritual part of ourselves so as to perceive a universal reality.

These studies do not dispel all mystery, but they do show that our brain needs the coherence provided by such beliefs in order to develop. According to the researchers, the more intense our perceptions, the greater our chance to survive, which is the ultimate goal of the brain's neurobiological work. To develop our brain, we must keep it alert. Wakeful dreaming is a pleasant way to do this. Recording the traces of our dreams enriches our understanding and lets us transmit that knowledge to others. It's a learning chain, the transmission of values by keeping our collective memory alive. By remaining conscious.

Let's dream the world and weave stories.

I was disappointed that I couldn't join my friend Michel Random in Rome. My ankle was still swollen and the trip was not a good idea. Luckily, it was a plentiful year for exhibitions in Paris.

Instead, I took advantage of my Parisian holiday to feast on culture and see some old friends. I realized how much I loved them. I knew that my work there would soon be done and I would have to move on, leaving wonderful memories.

During the final days of December, on waking, I would sip my coffee slowly, listening to the silence. It was my favorite time to transcribe yesterday's memories and thoughts into my journal. It was my way of stopping time, of keeping my memory alive.

One morning I heard the fax machine ring. In the weak, grayish winter light, a beautiful message was coming in, a message I slipped between two pages of my journal.

"We do not become old merely because we've lived a certain number of years. We become old when we've deserted our ideals. Years will wrinkle our skin; abandoning our ideals wrinkles the soul. Worries, doubts, fears and despair are enemies that slowly bend us toward the ground and turn us into dust before our deaths. He who can be astonished and marvel remains young. Like the insatiable child, he asks: and now? He defies events and finds joy in the game of life. You're as young as your faith, as old as your doubts, as young as your self-confidence, as old as your discouragement. You'll remain young as long as you remain open to the messages of nature, men and the infinite."

It was Isabelle who'd sent me these words by Winston Churchill because, reading them, she'd thought of me.

It was a few days before Christmas. I was grateful for her shared feelings.

A new year was about to begin and I felt like pursuing my ideal as far as possible. That morning, I felt unshakable confidence in the days to come, even though I had no idea in which country or projects it would take shape. I knew only that I would set out again in search of my desires so as to broaden my life.

Paris, December 2002

BOREAL MEDITATIONS

"We have to believe in the enormous potential of the human spirit, in its power to roam outside known and tangible frontiers. We have to believe in its ability to imagine, that is, to recreate forms, characters and even countries that will be born, inevitably, sooner or later."[1]

Jean Desy

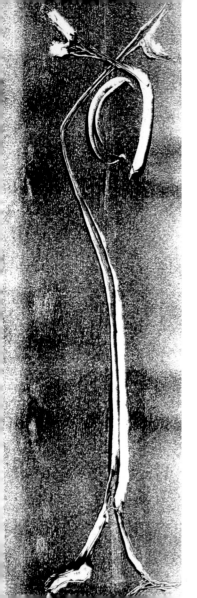

5

My French friends tease me because I'm so sensitive to cold. As though we were immune because we come from a cold country. Unfortunately, that's not so. I like the idea of the cold, but I can't really tolerate it. I shiver just to think of it.

But winter brings me more than the shivers; above all, it brings the pleasure of childhood memories, and special moments of reflection and meditation.

Early in the morning, the snow helps to produce an almost magical silence. Muffled. Soft. Enveloping. A silence that profoundly calms.

I love winter and its colors for the reverie they impart. I love to go for walks in powdery snow and blizzards. I love the fogs of winter dawns and evenings. But I also like to leave winter, the better to rediscover it. When it drags on for too long, sometimes until the end of March, I can't stand the waiting for spring any longer.

The last few years, I'd been particularly lucky. I would leave winter and return for short bouts, just long enough to appreciate and enjoy its real merits. But that particular winter, I was too busy in my city to leave for more than a few days. When I did get away, it was to go further north, even further into the cold.

I'd returned to Montreal in mid-January, when the cold is at its most intense and biting. My river was frozen, covered in ice and snow.

I'd come back because I had a project in northern Quebec, and another one that I was supposed to have completed by the new year but, to finish it properly, I had agreed to keep going for a few more months. I learned a big lesson in life from this last project. I realized that, in this case, my unfortunate tendency to say "yes" just to please people had cost me too much in terms of time.

The project lasted from October to March. My desire had vanished a long time ago, but I'd agreed to help a few people, and one in particular. My reluctance made me less than pleasant during those winter months. I felt I'd lost my freedom and was trapped in a ridiculous situation; it was my fault and kept me from accepting contracts in Europe.

Having ideas can be very absorbing, especially if you want to carry them out. But it becomes very difficult if you realize mid-way that you are risking your integrity, because of a lack of coherence between what you've proposed and what is actually taking place.

In the pursuit of an ideal, we sometimes find ourselves unwillingly participating in the sort of manipulation we're fighting against elsewhere. I felt I had to be wary.

George Steiner writes, in *Errata, An Examined Life,* that "our responses... are narratives of intuition."[2]

During the last few months, my impatient reactions, exasperation and unsmiling gaze spoke volumes about my intuitions. I realized that my obligation to my inner self was far more important than any sacrifice for others. For we don't always sacrifice ourselves for people who see clearly. We must each of us find our own road. It's a matter of personal integrity.

I was reminded of the novel by poet Jens Peter Jacobsen, *Marie Grubbe*, in which he draws the portrait of a woman who remained true to her inner self, even if her choices seemed difficult and ran counter to the customs and mores of her time. The character has the courage to remain true to her deep convictions throughout her life, even when it sets her on the most difficult social path. I say social, because it seems to me that, in the case of one's personal path, one has no choice. Constraints that block our forward progress usually come from the outside.

"Our feelings are not provoked by the interior of things, but by their appearance," writes Yves Simon in *The Drift of Feelings.* "The woman who's missing a tooth seems to be just a woman missing a tooth, yet that's insignificant in comparison to the size of her dreams."[3]

As for me, after years of being a consultant, I realized at last that I had to stop trying to change others. The only person I had to change was myself. The gaze I had to alter was mine. I understand this very well now, even though for a long time I didn't want to see or understand it, driven as I was by the crazy desire to change the world.

All that time, I'd stubbornly tried to change other people, thinking it was for their own good or for the good of society. I thought I could act from the outside. It may seem pretentious, but I assure you, my road was paved with the best intentions.

Happily, that winter I finally understood. The lesson had been a hard one for me, but enlightening. The lesson had been hard because I was always getting into situations that had nothing to do with who I was or, rather, with the person I'd become. Nor with my desires. I would agree to do something to please someone, or because I thought it would advance a greater cause, and thus increase others' awareness of what I considered essential.

I finally understood that we can only say these things to those who ask and are ready to hear them. Otherwise we're wasting our energy playing at Don Quixote, which I've done too often in my life. *Mea culpa.* But who said evolving was easy? I absorbed this life lesson like a transcendence. Even if I couldn't be sure that I wouldn't fall into the trap again in the first inattentive moment, I made the solemn resolution to do my best to put it into practice.

I had a premonition that, in the future, this new understanding would help me say *no* more easily. I realized that forgetting oneself for others was not the best way to give of oneself, that I had to continue to give as much, but without denying my own nature.

It was an important moment in my life, because I decided I would do no more consulting of the type I'd been doing. I would find another way. This simple realization freed me. When we force ourselves to give, those who receive seem incapable of gratitude. This angers us, especially since we made such an effort. I usually have no difficulty giving easily and willingly, but the few times when I did so unwillingly, those for whom the gift was intended seemed almost ungrateful, even petty.

I understood then that to give reluctantly, out of politeness or a sense of obligation, did no one any good. From now on, I would try to do everything wholeheartedly, and not out of duty (an often imaginary obligation we create ourselves).

I wanted to take advantage of my freedom to act in harmony with my conscience.

Thursday, January 23. We rose before dawn and headed for Baie Comeau. The night was ink black. As I looked out from inside the taxi, the dark sky made the snow seem even whiter.

At the airport, you could immediately identify people from the North, dressed in warm boots and bulky anoraks.

With our hoods, scarves and gloves, we were equipped to take on the great winds and northern cold. In spite of the early hour, travelers were smiling. Some talked among themselves over cups of coffee, others were bent over their newspapers.

The flight was on time. Boarding began on schedule. Ten minutes later the small airplane was full, every seat taken.

We barely had time to fasten our seatbelts before the plane took off into a clear blue sky, bordered by distant pink bands, traces of the sunrise over the white-powdered city.

It was warm in the airplane, but I didn't dare take my coat off. I was still half-asleep, and I let my eyelids shut out the pink sky. One hour and thirty-five minutes later, we were flying over the Manicouagan region.

As always, I held my breath at the sight of the broad expanses of blue water and the mountainsides of icy steel-gray granite covered, here and there, by immaculate snow. From our bird's eye view, everything was incredibly beautiful.

The lock on the door of our rented car was frozen. We had to wait for help.

The cold bit at our cheeks. My eyes were blurred with tears; my fingertips went numb inside my gloves.

The problem solved and the car loaded with computers, video projector and cameras, we took to the road at last.

It was lined with conifers, the only trees that can grow in boreal forests, having made their peace with the northern winds. The sun broke through the branches of spruce and fir. The rocks seemed immutable, unmoved by the passage of time. The sky was smooth as a stretched canvas. It was beautiful and calm.

We sped along in our American car until we reached Baie-Comeau Manor, where the seminar was being held. I was enthusiastic about this project. An entire region had decided to try the collective intelligence approach. In November, an initial appeal had been made to the population, inviting business people, civil servants and politicians to meet to reinvent the Manicouagan. They had responded to our call in good numbers.

We had come to facilitate a three-day seminar on leadership, for the first twenty-five people who registered. I had already given this seminar in French companies, and I wondered how the concept would be received in a region where participants came from different horizons. My seminars were, above all, creative workshops, and I was curious to see how entrepreneurs would react.

Once more, here was proof that, in a benevolent atmosphere, people can give the best of themselves. They can be truly creative.

They came up with terrific ideas, had a lot of fun, and now have a precious key in hand to reinvent their region: desire.

Seventy citizens dreamed of a region. These seventy citizens could then encourage others to dream, so that they would rely together on common values to build their civic space.

The Manicouagan region has chosen to trust their future to creative imagination, with the knowledge that, in a few years, we'll witness what they've done (or not) with their dreams if they decide to act.

In his *Guidelines for Man Today*, René Lenoir writes: "A man is a person, an autonomous subject, open to others, capable of creating forms and meanings. His creations can do more than combine pre-existing elements; he can bring forth something new, unexpected. This idea is consistent with Aristotle, Kant and, more recently, Castoriadis: we must constantly reinvent society through use of creative imagination in perpetual dialogue with the universe of values. This universe is incessantly in motion, even if the movement is barely perceptible; we sense it is driven by an invisible force, at work in our consciousness."[4]

I was thrilled by their creativity. Their consciousness had been awakened; the work was underway. Anything was possible if they stayed the course. I hope their determination will resist the pressures of time and other constraints. The future will tell. Their performance indicator: the creation of 5,000 new jobs in the next ten years. I hope they won't wait for help from governments or big business to act. I hope they will be their own creators.

We always experience euphoric moments when we're setting the process in motion, but sometimes the project runs out of steam when it has to wrestle with daily constraints. Who's to blame? Often it's time itself, or rather what we've done with it. Sometimes there's a lack of organization, sometimes a lack of vision. We get lost in details and forget what's essential: the objective we gave ourselves so we could realize our dream. Sometimes also a degree of laziness sets in, as our desires and courage to act become exhausted. We fall unconsciously into a kind of torpor, allowing sterile political maneuvering to gain ground. When that happens, we rarely attain our projected results. The key is to maintain a spirit of solidarity day by day.

The strength of collective leadership in action is the complementarity of individual intelligences and talents. It is expressed in a thousand ways:

One person takes on new tasks in the absence of another, so that the process continues unabated. Mutual confidence and solidarity allow the project to move forward without exhausting the team members. A natural climate of mutual aid sets in.

Strength comes from the continual learning chain by which dreams, desires, knowledge, creations and stories are shared, so that everyone remains in the loop and knows exactly what the situation is, so that they can contribute for the best. It comes from transparency and communication.

Strength comes too from sharing power, the hardest aspect to achieve. It comes from allowing each participant to practice their leadership in accordance with their talents, experience and contribution to the project; this allows each individual to act in a concrete and useful manner that is then recognized by all.

The strength of collective leadership is expressed by the quality of follow-up and wide circulation of results, of what has been accomplished.

And finally, that strength leads to the assumption of collective responsibility, which is only achieved if we avoid the trap of giving responsibility only to the same person or committee.

Everyone must get involved; everyone has to appropriate some part of the dream and its achievement.

The secret is simple: everyone must feel responsible. We can win everyone's commitment as long as everyone obtains their share of pleasure and self-improvement. Isn't that what the Athenians did when they created democracy?

That winter I forgot the cold. From my many trips to that boreal region of Manicouagan, I retain a memory of the desire of a few citizens to turn their remoteness into a strength. They set me dreaming.

The people of the Manicouagan gave me hope, and I felt the echo of the words of Jean-Paul Sartre at the end of his life: "Hope means that I can't undertake an action without assuming I'll accomplish it… Action, which has hope in it, cannot, from the start, be doomed to failure… There is in hope a kind of necessity…"[5]

I believe this hope is shared by those I met on the shores of that great northern bay.

Each new experience refines my approach and confirms my initial hypotheses: art heals and brings people together.

As sociologist Jean-Louis Bernard explains in the published proceedings of a colloquium on artistic creation and the dynamics of insertion: "The form is as important as the content. One becomes autonomous only if one is recognized by others as an actor, and if one recognizes oneself as an actor."[6]

When we create a book, a play or a performance, we always feel as though we're building ourselves. The same should be true for any act, because acts of creation are the noblest acts a human being can accomplish.

In an art-therapy approach, "we move from a system of assistance to a system of actors. People are not considered to be empty and ignorant (without experience or culture); on the contrary, we begin by building on their experience, competences and culture."[7]

Artistic creation emancipates us because it brings a spirit of liberty and moments of transcendence. It allows us to hear that small inner voice of perpetual metamorphosis. When placed in the service of a collective project, it becomes the power of creative imagination.

Artistic creation combined with a collective intelligence process represents the best tool for carrying out projects that are both strategic and sustainable.

That winter, I discovered a new face of beauty in the world.

I spent a long time gazing at the polar shores that stretched as far as the eye could see, majestic.

Then there were those narrow snow-covered paths along the mountainsides where, one Sunday morning, I came across a young man with his Dalmatian. With its black spots on white, the dog seemed to have been created especially to match this forest, a forest that might have come straight out of childhood fairytales.

Large downy flakes fell softly on snow-covered fir trees. My footsteps left the first traces of the day on the ground. Occasionally the silence was broken by the song of a bird.

The magic gave me a taste for northern destinations I will keep forever.

What I propose during my seminars is to advance and live in the creation of beauty. All I do is play along with the participants. We play at dreaming, miming, drawing, painting, closing our eyes, inventing stories, rehearsing and putting on a play. We play at creating to invent beauty.

"… men nourish themselves as much on stories as on bread," writes Jean Desy. "Always stories. We have a real need for dreaming, reverie, literature and artistic activity. Human beings need stories to maintain their spirits, to better integrate their experiences and give them meaning…"[8]

We must be careful of the world we build, the world we inundate with images and noise. We have to be careful to leave some empty space for our imaginations to create if we hope to continue the game of stories.

Dante associated literary creation with inspired visions that came to him like a rain of images. It seems to me that we should be careful to leave some virgin spaces in our children's imaginations so they too can close their eyes and experience a rain of images.

Those moments of silence are critical. Kundera lamented, about the sound of the radio, that "it persecutes us in the cafés, restaurants, trains, even during our visits to people who have become incapable of living without nonstop feeding of the ears."[9]

If all of us could commit ourselves each year to create, alone or with our family, the stillness and silences necessary to create one small thing that seems beautiful to us, that small gesture could eventually turn us into multipliers of beauty.

I truly believe that beauty can save the world. It's much stronger than we think. Even though wars constantly destroy it, it reappears to astonish and move us. We just have to lend an ear or turn our gaze to a small corner of nature as yet unspoiled by man, or to a work of art, where the great mysteries of creation are still intact.

One way to do battle would be to dedicate ourselves to inventing beauty with as much determination as those determined to destroy it.

And we can also better acquaint ourselves with the beauty that already exists, like in this scene from Yves Simon's novel:

"They thought that, tonight or tomorrow, they might die, or others would go to their deaths, but first it was necessary… You hear me! It was necessary that a man, a woman, two more human beings discover a few words written by Dante, Apollinaire or Rimbaud…

"That's what I call beauty in this world, that secret effort, synonymous with raising oneself up. And that's what the black boots of war wanted to annihilate, the beauty of this world. The very memory of that beauty…"[10]

Isn't our struggle one to conserve beauty at all costs: to conserve its memory by recounting beauty to each other, to make it known by sharing our discoveries, to protect beauty wherever it already exists and to invent it anew?

Light up the night. The present situation may be dark, but it can turn rosy just as the night sky does at dawn. Writing this, I'm dreaming of alchemical transformations and new founding myths.

As a Westerner and child of this era, I have an unfortunate tendency to be Manichean.

Things are black or white, good or bad, and I have difficulty imagining they can be both at once. In life, however, it's different. It's always a little bit of both at the same time. One can't exist without the other.

I know this in theory, but I'm still a long way from the Chinese wisdom that teaches us that "yin and yang are opposite, but they are also interdependent: one cannot exist without the other. Everything contains opposing forces that constantly depend on each other. Night is the opposite of day, but there would be no night without day. Action cannot exist without rest, energy without matter, compression without expansion."[11]

At times we have to accept the dark side of things to discover light there. Life teaches us this everyday. Often bad news rains down, and we're left feeling that there's no way out. Then the situation turns around completely.

That's why, despite current trends, I still have hope that everything is possible. My enthusiastic nature leads me to adopt a combative attitude, ready for battle; when the goal seems too high, I wait for a sign and remain confident, letting fate slowly but surely do its work. To succeed in walking that fine line, between taking flight and waiting, represents, to me, the great complexity of life.

I try to fill those periods of waiting with well-nourished reveries, knowing that sooner or later they will be translated into reality or be replaced by new, more essential desires.

It's my way of transcending, by wakeful dreaming, the aspects of my life that don't satisfy me. I like the idea of transcending them, because I still hope they'll evolve one day, even though I know I can't do anything about it.

There are aspects of our lives we don't control. Isn't that what makes life so exciting?

"To be born is, in a sense, to be promised to a promise, to a future that palpitates before us though we can't see it. So long as the face of the future remains unknown," notes Pascal Bruckner, "that promise has a price. It's in the nature of freedom, that it marshals existence where we don't expect it, that it outwits biological and sociological determinations. The excitement of not knowing what tomorrow will bring, the uncertainty of what awaits us, is by far superior to the regularity of those pleasures inscribed in our cells."[12]

We each negotiate our life in our own way. I like extremes. I find my balance by integrating my polarities. Just as I can be intensely happy in the present at one moment, I can struggle to transcend another instant, because suffering hits me with the same intensity of emotion. It's the passion of living, holding moments both gentle and grave.

That's why it's with a hint of a smile, seeing myself in each verse, that I sing the words of Carla Bruni's "*The Excessive*" to myself: "It's just that existence, without a bit of the extreme, is missing something."[13]

I appreciate life as it is, but I'm convinced that my gaze and my senses help to make each moment more intense, more magical.

It's a question of "being in the world," Michel Maffesoli says in *The Eternal Instant,* where he proclaims the return of the tragic in postmodern societies: "… non-action is in no way passive," he writes. "It enacts another strategy toward people and things. It doesn't merely follow the *via recta* of reason — which may be undeniably efficient, but only in the short term — it takes a more complex path, that of passion, of the emotions in which all human existence is steeped.[14]

We have to live life fully for what it is, while nourishing our desires so as to develop the drive to surpass ourselves and realize our dreams. In his essay on happiness, Pascal Bruckner states: "Happiness stems as much from immediate pleasure as from hope in a project capable of revealing new sources of happiness."[15] Leaving a lot of room in our lives for emotions does not mean eliminating reason. We can appreciate the efficiency of a well-run project. We should use reason for what it offers us. But the risk increases with abuse.

We have a natural tendency to excess. And I'm no exception; I can be very rational and efficient. "A woman of results," people will tell you. But life has taught me something: there's a price to pay for being too rational.

There's also a price to pay when you divide life in two, putting evil on one side and good on the other. We often do the same with ourselves. We have trouble accepting our mistakes and weaknesses.

We have to learn to develop a critical sense without destroying ourselves, or others. Today, I look as much for the dark side as the light, in myself first, and then in others.

I look for meaning as much as results. It's a difficult quest, but never boring. We are at once a part and the whole. Our actions participate in the unity of the world.

Integration is not easy. The ideal would be to be able to integrate imminence — suspending movement, concentrating on the self — and transcendence — sharing dreams, taking collective action and pride in realizing common projects, and communing with the world. It's a constant oscillation between movement and non-movement, between self-creation and collective creation.

It's this movement of life we must rediscover within organizations, to introduce a rhythm and a degree of disorder to make them livelier.

"… as soon as anything is imperfect, it is bountiful," writes Michel Maffesoli. Perfection is a sign of death. Wherever there's friction — opposition, dispute, disorder — there's vitality. Cultural and scientific works are often created in disorder and folly. Or, to put it in more academic terms, the conjunction of the spiritual and the natural sciences is both the cause and the effect of a veritable cultural upheaval…"[16]

Therein lies my crazy hope to reverse the current trend. Since the world is in such disorder, isn't there an opportunity for renewed enchantment? And couldn't beauty be the key?

Jean Hurstel, from the *Centre européen de la jeune création* (European Center for Emerging Creation) in Strasbourg, states: "To close or to open. To exercise the imagination is to exercise collective freedom for the greatest number, and not only for the creator. Exercising this collective freedom necessarily means going further than the consequences, and returning to the political and social causes of the present disaster."[17]

I've been developing this collective intelligence and artistic creation approach for a number of years now, but I'm always happy to come upon texts and commentaries that confirm my hypotheses. It's very encouraging to see that other experiences undertaken in completely different contexts arrive at the same conclusions.

It's one more proof that the unity of the world does exist, and that it is worthwhile for each of us to contribute our best, our best creation.

As Castoriadis puts it, "… the true reception of a new work is as creative as its creation."[18]

We should be open to each other, and encourage each other to create as authors, and to receive as audiences. It's our responsibility to create a climate of emulation and to transform public places into intellectual and creative greenhouses, to build our society together.

I was relieved to see the end of March. I'd finished the contract that had been weighing so heavily on me. At last, I'd turned the page and, I hoped, learned my lesson.

I regretted my impatience and mood swings. I had only myself to blame for the extended time it took to fulfill the contract.

I should have assumed the consequences of my "yes" with more elegance. Unfortunately, from time to time, I'd taken my frustration out on others. I knew that.

I also understood that, by respecting my inner self, I might avoid making the same mistake again. Maybe, at last, I'd learned to say no.

That year, winter dragged on. I walked through the snow-covered streets of Old Montreal, promising myself to try to be happy so I could radiate it. When we're unhappy, we project our anguish and unhealthy frustration on others. Nobody asks us to say yes at such a cost. The spirit of sacrifice is an illusion.

Doesn't everyone prefer smiles to funereal faces? I think beauty is best appreciated with a smile. When we frown too much, beauty and happiness tend to escape us.

From now on I had a duty to be free and happy, and to avoid anything that could make me stray from my path.

Montreal, Baie Comeau, January – March 2003

ACTS OF BEAUTY

"Ugliness: we practice it because we don't see beauty sufficiently."[1]

Ingres

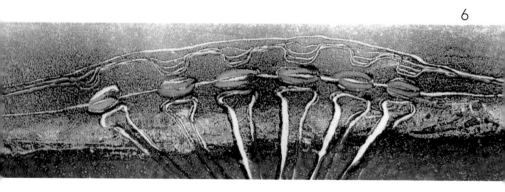

6

It was mid-April. Still the snow and cold lingered in Quebec. It was as though spring would never come. I was surprised and relieved to find Paris in the midst of a heat wave at Easter. I switched directly from woolen sweaters to linen blouses, without the slightest step in between. Surprisingly, after the long cold months, I found it difficult to drop my layers of clothing. It was as though my skin had retained the memory of my winter shivering.

I'd decided to drop everything and think for a while. I hadn't even had time to set foot in Paris for the last three months. It was no longer worth keeping an apartment there.

After my four-year adventure, I was leaving my Paris apartment.

I couldn't believe how much I'd accumulated. In four years, I'd managed to fill the cupboards with all and sundry; it took several days to sort through what would stay in France and what was going back to Quebec.

I found photos, messages, postcards. I began to reread notebook entries. My heart ached at having to leave. I wandered in the disorder I had created with a twinge of melancholy.

Whenever I was in Paris, I would see my friends as time allowed. That Sunday, I told a friend that I'd hardly had time to enjoy Paris because of my moving preparations. I was leaving in two days to attend a conference. It was our last chance to celebrate, and it had to be magical. Especially since I didn't know when I'd be back.

We set out in a Parisian drizzle, without a clear idea of what we were going to do.

We crossed the Champs-Élysées and walked along the small streets down to the Seine. We stopped for lunch on the patio of L'Avenue restaurant. It was still early. The jet-set fauna were still in their beds. The place was almost empty, which was very pleasant.

A large, magnificent maroon-colored dog greeted us. He had beautiful ochre eyes and seemed to know his way around the personnel. As far as adoring attention was concerned, he was the uncontested center of attention.

Through the window, the wide Avenue Montaigne was almost deserted. A fine rain was falling under a gray sky. We were happy to be together.

After an excellent meal, we continued our walk. I was surprised to see no one in front of the Grand Palais. I'd tried to visit the Chagall exhibition, but in vain; the lineups were always too long. That Sunday, by luck, we walked right in, and took advantage of the relatively empty rooms to truly appreciate *Chagall: Known and Unknown.* I was happy to discover that my desire, which I'd practically given up on, was satisfied. To leave Paris without some kind of cultural nourishment would have saddened me.

We continued our walk, crossing the 7th Arrondissement by way of Les Invalides, and following small streets into the 6th. The rain had ceased; the sky was a clear, restful gray.

My friend showed me the building where she'd lived close by the Rodin Museum, saying, "A person can be very unhappy in a very luxurious apartment. I'm a thousand times happier now, living in my little room."

We began to come across people strolling. The sun made occasional brief appearances through the clouds. Around 4 p.m., we stopped for tea and a short rest in a charming little hotel on Saint Germain.

I knew I would retain a happy memory of this long walk in Paris. Wandering in that city, when the crowds are not too bad, is one of my favorite pleasures. Meanwhile, the rain had started coming down again.

We walked as far as the Louvre, crossing the gardens and passing in front of the Comédie Française to finally pause in Saint Roch Church on rue Saint Honoré.

My friend wanted to show me the Chapel of Saint Rita, the virgin of lost causes to whom she had prayed so often when she had been in difficulty. We both sat on a bench in the back of the Chapel to hear the silence and gather our thoughts.

I shut my eyes and breathed in the smell of the old stones. Soon after, we heard very beautiful gospel singing. We got up to see who was singing. There were at least twenty singers in the nave, rocking gracefully, their arms raised to the sky, each waving a white handkerchief in his or her right hand. It was lovely. It looked like a choreography of black and white swans. I stole a glance at my friend. Her tearful eyes betrayed her emotion. It's true that those songs went straight to your heart. It was a moment of pure beauty. I thought how wonderful that it happened just as we'd come into the church. It was the kind of pure beauty described by Dominique Fernandez: "Pure beauty must be impersonal and timeless; it must not belong in any way to whoever created it, or at least it must not seem to belong to them."[4]

At the start of the day, my heart full of the desire for beauty, I'd called on magic to intervene. And now the day was passing gently, with small touches, here and there, of the marvelous.

We started back in the half-light. Twilight illuminated the narrow streets. We walked to the Place Vendôme to listen to a harp and drink a glass of champagne. Looking at the bubbles, I made a secret vow to invent a life for myself with this much sparkle. A few streets from there, we ended the evening with a light dinner at the Hotel Coste, in a small, intimate, candlelit room with walls covered in burgundy silk. Walking back to my apartment, I slowed my pace near the Champs-Élysées. I wanted to retain in my memory every detail of that night, every shadow, every sound, every scent. I knew it would be some time before I could enjoy Paris again.

Two days later, as I cast a final glance around the empty apartment I was leaving, this time for good, I remembered the evening that Jacques had stopped by the equally empty apartment with a bottle of champagne and two glasses to celebrate my arrival on his street. Now, on this late morning in April, the adventure was ending.

In the taxi on the way to the airport, I suddenly felt terribly sad; I realized how attached I'd become to my friends and my Parisian life. I knew I'd be back, but I didn't know when. I was leaving for an unknown destination.

I looked at the other passengers in the airplane, and wondered what we had in common. I recalled the words of Hubert Reeves: "Does the idea of meeting someone who changes your life make sense at all?"[5]

Each of us has been in situations or had personal experiences that seemed to involve a kind of synchronicity.

Such as meeting someone essential, whom we could have missed altogether, by mere seconds. We have all felt these signs, faint but so symbolic, that can seem like answers to the questions we're asking ourselves. Because we're not used to thinking this way, we wonder if we aren't imagining things, seeing signs where there are none.

"Do personal experiences have any meaning," writes Kundera, "beyond the fact of their occurrence? Despite my considerable skepticism, I still have a trace of irrational superstition, such as the strange idea that everything that happens to me has some meaning, signifies something. I think that, as it passes, life speaks to us, gradually revealing some secret, offering itself as a rebus to decipher. Events, as they happen to us, make up a mythology of our lives, and I believe that this mythology contains the key to truth and mystery. An illusion? Possibly, even likely, but I can't repress the need to continually decipher my own life."[6]

If I hadn't received a phone call from a woman offering me a job in July 1986, I would never have met the colleague who, later, in March 1987, introduced me to the man of my life.

If I hadn't had a phone call from a client in the spring of 1989, inviting me to a meeting with an American looking for a consultant to carry out an urgent project, I would never have undertaken my projects for the multinational Alumax, and would never have been able to write *City of Intelligences*. If Michel Coutu had not brought a copy of *City* to France and given it to the Director of the Center for Research and Study for CEO's, I would never have lived in Paris, or met all those exceptional people who contributed to my growth. If I hadn't written *City,* I certainly wouldn't be writing *School of Desires* at this moment. And so on. Everything is connected.

When you think about it, our lives are made of a series of encounters that change our lives. How could they not have meaning?

"These events, Jung tells us, are not isolated, but belong to 'a universal factor existing throughout eternity'... The psychic factor that Jung associates with events deemed 'synchronous' is not added onto some impersonal Nature. It is a sign of the great unity of our universe on every front. Are such speculations futile and dense?" asks Hubert Reeves. "I don't think so. They're more likely intuitions clumsily expressed. Even words fail us."[7]

Knowing that we're all linked, imagine what we could do if we encouraged each other to participate more fully in the entirety of the world. It's amazing what a difference each of us could make if we were united instead of divided. We could view problems from a global perspective by building links between each other because we are already all connected. **We are influenced by our surroundings.**

As Michel Maffesoli reminds us so well, "… life's inner logic is a 'hierarchical chain,' so that, in all of nature and society, each part has no meaning on its own, but only in relation with others. It's no longer a question of a simple addition of equal individuals forming a social contract, but rather a far more concrete and solid organic synergy. It's not a question of dichotomies either, such as good or evil, darkness or light, justice or injustice. Though such dichotomies have marked the modern world, their attraction is fading. The tragic, by placing these different elements in relation to each other, refers to their conjunctions, to a famed *coincidentia oppositorum bine* more difficult to think and live but much more concrete and rooted in the human. It is the humble acceptance of what introduces each and every one of us into the entirety of the world where we each can find refuge and the opportunity to grow, and which, at the same time, can show each of us the intrinsic value of this world's existence."[8]

If being oneself is being in the world, it's already a first step toward participating fully.

The Dalai Lama says that even the seemingly most violent person, the most evil, can feel happiness when they show compassion toward another. This belief is not only held by religious leaders. Tolstoy shared it. He believed that goodness could triumph over evil.

I too want to believe it. Just as I believe that beauty can triumph over ugliness.

Why couldn't fraternity be developed by training? We need to experience compassion to realize how beneficial it really is. The feeling that we are making a difference for someone else is certainly one of the great joys of life. We see this in crisis situations. Everyone finds comfort in making their small contribution to those in distress. What can be discouraging sometimes is the enormity of the task, or the misappropriation of good intentions.

At last… we face this planetary disorder and, at the same time, a universe full of all possibilities. I wonder what we might invent in our imaginations, that territory of vast open spaces, to build new connections.

"There is a link between realizing that life is short, and the inalienable right to sensuality and beauty. What's more, the stability of the Greek city-state rests essentially on the possibility for everyone to get the most from that sensuality," adds Michel Maffesoli.[9]

We ought to borrow the eyes of Ulysses to embrace the future with eagerness and curiosity. Like him, we should see before us an enormous unexplored territory. Like him, we should vigorously feed our desire. Desire to dream. Desire to learn. Desire to accomplish. Desire to give.

What would you say if I invited you to put your computer screens and electronic agendas on sleep? Asked you to close your eyes? Would you be willing to sit still for a few minutes, to try out immobility and take the time to imagine a new world?

If your answer is yes, I would like the pages of this book to be interactive so that I could hear your silence and your sighs. I would love to transcribe your dreams to turn them into one single dream. A great dream. The dream of tomorrow.

You may think it's completely crazy. I agree. Being in the world does not exclude folly, quite the contrary… To make my life a personal work of art, to make the world a collective work of art, that's my dream. If you think I'm a fabulist, I agree. Therein lies my happiness. I'm even convinced that the craziest among you will accomplish the extraordinary. It's something I'd love to witness. I'd like it to be contagious so that we would be very many to play this imaginary game, to create parcels of reality.

To enchant the world, create new founding myths, engender collective thinking, powerful and irresistible, we must be a great many fabulists. Let's be Ulysses and explore the territories of our collective unconscious, with the drive to create a new fraternal world — regardless of religion.

It seems to me that such a fundamental value should unite us regardless of our beliefs, and contribute to reducing wars.

Inevitably there will be failures, disappointments, disillusionments. But what would it cost us to try? Just to try. This game might actually bring us a bit of pleasure and happiness, merely in the attempt to build something.

When I see the means that are sometimes used to defend beautiful ideals, I fear for humankind. I choose the collective dream rather than mass manipulation. I prefer to associate the female and male spirits rather than to set them against each other.

I'm suspicious of beautiful speeches that hide an unhealthy and megalomaniac power, which kills fraternity. I have more faith in gentleness to humanize the hard-hearted. I'm suspicious of irony and cynicism; look where they've brought us so far. I'd rather put my faith in beauty.

"Our ears and our eyes are weary; it's our hearts that must be touched," Gandhi said.

I have no particular method to propose beyond an approach based on collective intelligence and artistic creation. I would prefer to entice you into a game of wandering without any specific goal, in which we'd take whichever paths we happened upon, as though we were on a walk through the woods, far from the beaten track. I'm not a good guide; I tend to get lost. My fertile imagination has so many paths to propose. In action, I only know how to proceed by trial and error.

All I possess is a great desire that takes the form of a wakeful dream, as I put it into words and images.

All I have is an intuition, sometimes imperceptible, sometimes so present that it pushes me toward you for a great meeting of imaginations.

All I fear is my passion, which makes me so impatient to witness a real renaissance in society. Before I die.

We rejected the myths of the Middle Ages because of their abuse of superstitions. We've now completed two centuries of excessive rationalism. Isn't it time for a new meeting of emotion and reason, image and words, myths and thought, memory and imagination? Isn't it time to rely on integration?

Our technical and scientific knowledge have served progress well. Could our imagination serve the cause of humanity with equally impressive positive results? If only we could enchant the world again.

I say this because, like Georges Steiner, "… I am unable, even at the worst hours, to abdicate from the belief that the two validating wonders of mortal existence are love and the invention of the future tense."[10]

And I know that I'm not alone in this conviction. Many of you share it.

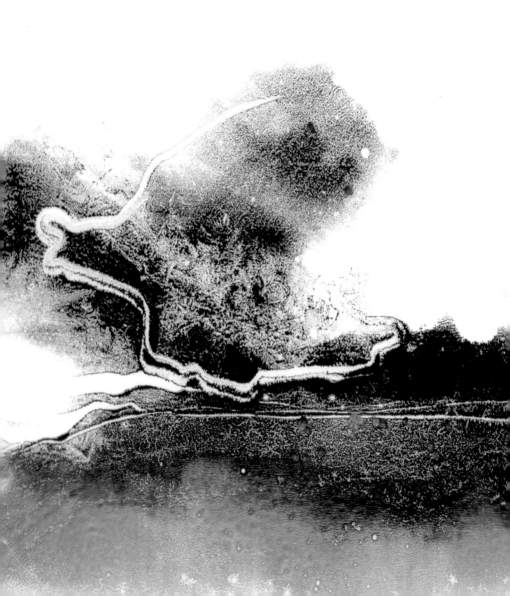

The poet Christian Bobin says that, on his own, he is foolish. He needs another in order to think, to understand. He needs to write because writing calls up another force. I too believe we all need others, even though we're quite good at separation, disunity and killing each other.

"The new forms of communication and information don't necessarily facilitate human interaction: Each of us is seated alone in front of our computer screen, and even when many of us watch the same TV program, our gazes remain parallel and have no opportunity to meet. Some people seek a solution in religion, but religions don't always bring people together, since each of us can choose our own from among the enormous repertoire spanning centuries and civilizations. Children may not bring themselves up yet, but often they have a single parent, or alternate between two. This growing solitude," explains Tzvetan Todorov, "this social autism, does not lead, as might be expected, to greater differentiation between individuals but, rather, to the opposite. Even

Montaigne understood this: taken in isolation, humans are alike; it's their constellations that are unique, unlike each other. Freedom is illusory when people's behaviors follow the same trends and seek to conform to the same images."[11]

I believe that choosing a collective intelligence and creative approach modeled on artists could help us to create beautiful constellations while reinforcing individual identities.

We have to organize spaces that foster development of individual and collective strategies. We should take inspiration from collaborative creation in art to transform our projects and experiments into liberating exercises that bring people together.

"The exercise of collective freedom is accomplished naturally by a process of surpassing the clichés and stereotypes of social norms that we have internalized," Jean Hurstel tells us.

"This process of surpassing is called sublimation. It's by sublimation and transference that the alchemical transformation operates in a process, project or artistic adventure."[12]

With the collective intelligence artistic approach, we must put our faith in humanism, as defined by Todorov in his *Imperfect Garden,* a book we would do well to keep close at hand in the times to come, because it will help us to work harder, in all our actions, to give life to the modern humanist world view:

"Humanism is, firstly, a concept of Man, an anthropology. It is not rich in content. It is limited to three traits: that all humans and exclusively humans belong to the same biological species; that they are social, that is, mutually dependent not only in order to feed themselves and reproduce, but also to become conscious and speaking beings; and finally, that they are relatively undetermined, therefore able to make different choices, thus forming their own collective history or biography, and responsible for their cultural or individual identity. These traits — or this 'human nature,' if you will — are not in themselves valued; but when humanists add a morality and politics to this minimal anthropology, they select values in conformity to this 'nature,' rather than the purely artificial products of an arbitrary will. Here, nature and freedom are no longer opposed. It's the case of the universality of the 'they,' the finality of the 'you,' and the autonomy of the 'I.' Indeed, the three pillars of the humanist morality are the recognition of equal dignity for all the members of the species, the elevation of the particular human being other than me to the ultimate goal of my action and, finally, the preference of the freely chosen action over action undertaken by constraint.

"None of these values can be reduced to any other; they can even, at times, be opposed one to the other. What characterizes the humanist doctrine is, in fact, their interaction, not the mere presence of one or the other. The praise for freedom and the desire for sovereignty are also present in other doctrines, individualist or scientistic. In humanism, they are limited by the finality of the 'you' and the universality of the 'they': I prefer to exercise my personal freedom rather than be satisfied with obeying, but only if that exercise does not harm anyone else (the freedom of my fist ends at the cheek of my neighbor, John Stuart Mill used to say, in a spirit shared by humanists); I want my State to be independent, but that does not give it the right to subjugate other States. Autonomy is a freedom contained in fraternity and equality. Nor are 'you' and 'they' equivalent. As citizens, all members of a society are interchangeable, and their relations are governed by justice, which is grounded in equality. As individuals, those same people are absolutely irreducible one to the other, and what counts is their difference, not their equality; the relations that arise between them require preferences, affection and love.

"Humanists do not 'believe' in Man, nor do they sing his praises. They know, first of all, that men cannot do everything, that they are limited by their very plurality, since the desires of some only rarely coincide with those of others; by their history and culture, which they do not choose; and by their physical being, whose limits are rapidly attained. Most of all, they know that men are not necessarily good, that they are even capable of the worst. The harm they have inflicted on each other during the 20th century is present in our memories, and makes any hypothesis based on the idea of human goodness untenable; in fact, proof that dismisses such an idea has never been lacking. Yet it's precisely in the midst of the horrors of war and the camps that the modern humanists, Primo Levi, Romain Gary, Vassily Grossman made their choice and affirmed their faith in the human capacity to also act freely, to also do good. Modern humanism, far from ignoring Auschwitz and Kolyma, stems from them; it is neither proud, nor naïve.

"If we adhere both to the idea of indetermination and to that of shared values, there is a path that connects them; we call it education. Men are not good, but they can become good: this is the very broad meaning of the educational process, of which school instruction is only a small part. In the modern Western world, and this too is recent, most children are no longer produced by chance; they are, as a rule, wanted. As a result, the responsibility of all those who can influence the transformation of children into free adults capable of solidarity is increased: of their family first, but also of their school and of society as a whole. The goal is not merely to ensure children's survival, nor even to facilitate their success, but to allow them to discover the loftiest pleasures. To achieve this, it is necessary to cultivate certain traits and marginalize others, rather than being content with approving them all, simply because they're there."[13]

School of Desires

In short, we all have a dream to create, a role to play in the production of this societal history. When will our life become a building block in this humanist construction? When will the unreal become real? When will our fantastical desire become our society? I don't know. I am certain, however, that the desires, dreams and acts of each one of us are examples that make a small difference. As these acts increase and complement each other, we will make a bigger difference.

Enacting Beauty. It was already May. Montreal was finally free of snow.

The cold had lingered so long that it had left hardly any time for the smells of spring, the mix of cool and warm breezes.

It felt as though we'd gone straight from wintry cold snaps to summer heat waves.

I finished my contracts, organized my files and prepared my retreat from the world by giving my friends notice to forget me for the summer.

I couldn't let myself be distracted by festivities and lounging around. I had to keep procrastination at bay.

This time my head was brimming after a period of gestation that had already lasted several months. I had to stop and give birth to it.

I intended to interrupt my professional activities for six months to write this book.

That was as much time as I could go without income. Even six months was already a long time. I told myself I would try to make it my act of beauty, my small contribution for the year.

I'd thought about it for several weeks. I was looking for something I could do immediately. I had several ideas and big dreams for the future but I didn't yet have the means to carry them out.

I was still confident I would accomplish them someday. In the meantime, the book project seemed to be the most accessible. A small building block in the construction of the edifice.

In the space of several months, three acts of beauty had attracted my attention and greatly impressed me.

I decided to make them my three stars in the summer nights of solitude I was preparing to experience.

I told myself that, on days when I felt too lonely, I would take courage by thinking of the artisans of these three acts.

Placed side by side, these stories provide a very attractive view of the world. They represent, for me, what the images of Steinberg did for Roland Barthes.

A prolific and inventive critic, Roland Barthes would look at artist-painter Steinberg's images and wonder:

"How can a picture give us ideas? Steinberg's certainly do. Or rather — something more precious — he makes us want to have ideas," Barthes said.[14]

For my part, I'd like to share these stories that give us the desire — or better still — make us want to have desires.

BEAUTY - FIRST ACT

Once upon a time... a man earned his living as a barber. In 1967, long hair became fashionable. Unable to feed his three children on his income from barbering, he became a school janitor, a job he did for thirty years, twelve of them at Denise Pelletier School in Rivière des Prairies in Quebec.

It was a job, writes Rima Elkouri, Montreal journalist at *La Presse*, that fit him like a glove. "He was sturdy, attentive, accessible, always available and very discreet. Everyone confided in him: children, parents and teachers. He was the sort who knew everything about everyone, but never gossiped."

Every morning, he got up at 3:45 a.m. to bring his wife to work; at 6:30 a.m., he opened the school doors and prepared to welcome everyone with a smile.

"I lived with him for forty years and I never saw him in a bad mood in the morning," his wife told Elkouri.

Bernard could not bear to see a child cry. In his office, he kept "spare socks, everything you needed to repair a zipper, etc… He was like everyone's grandfather. Bernard could solve every problem, big or small."

They would send him the difficult children that the teachers couldn't manage. "He was a psycho-educator, a specialized teacher and an excellent counselor, all in one," Raoul Absi, principal of the school confided.

Bernard Comtois retired at the age of 58. On his final day, the 500 students of the school were gathered in the gym.

"The teachers formed a guard of honor. They all sang for the janitor, who was overwhelmed.

The principal told him that the teachers' staff room, where he'd washed the dishes every day, would now bear his name. He was flattered and embarrassed."[15]

Bernard died on December 24, 2002, following a heart attack. In telling his story, journalist Rima Elkouri made us want to desire.

The example was especially beautiful because it contrasted so sharply with the usual stream of bad news in the media.

Bernard transformed his life into acts of beauty, acts that were appreciated by the children and recognized by all.

Each act counts, and those that bear witness to these acts also awaken our desires.

Reading this story in the newspaper that morning brightened my day. I, in turn, told it to others, who never failed to smile.

For my part, I decided that, whenever I felt like complaining, I would think of Bernard. And smile.

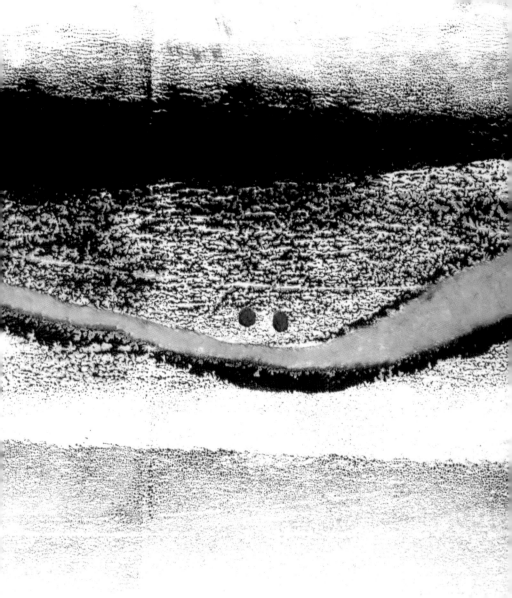

BEAUTY - SECOND ACT

I first heard about this next story in the winter of 2002. I'd had the idea to transform a client's annual report on sustainable development into a magazine on that same theme. We agreed on an innovative way to do it: we would invite employees in the various regions to write the articles.

Employees of each plant were asked to find interesting subjects on the themes of environment, energy, life at work and in the community.

As editor-in-chief, I was especially touched by an article written by Gilles Chassé of the Baie Comeau plant about a company called Norfil.

By chance, a year later, I was in Baie Comeau to lead a seminar on leadership. I realized that one of the participants was Claude Belzile, president and founder of Norfil. Naturally, I asked to visit his company.

I wanted to meet his team, who were guided by a concept similar to my collective intelligence approach. I wasn't disappointed. Far from it.

It was eloquent proof that, when we respect people and rely on their intelligence and culture, the results can be amazing.

That day, unbeknownst to me, I had a rendezvous with beauty. I was already familiar with the beauty of the landscape, but the beauty I was to witness was subtler. It was hidden within four walls. And the story was even more beautiful than I had thought possible.

Once upon a time… there was a man with a huge dream. In his youth he thought he might study architecture, but after attending his first classes in Montreal, he decided it wasn't for him. Several weeks later, he was back in his native northern region of Quebec.

He took a job as a mental health educator in the residential and long-term care hospital in Baie Comeau, where he met an extraordinary co-worker with whom he collaborated for ten years, Marie-Claude Lafrance.

Together, they thought of and tried ways to help patients feel more stable, more autonomous and happier. It was during that time that he first dreamed of creating a workplace adapted to the developmental needs of his patients.

Having reached the limit of what could be done in a hospital to help the development of intellectually challenged patients, he wanted to find a way to help them become more autonomous.

He did research, visited achievement centers in many regions, and then began to draw up a business plan to create a company that would hire such people.

He shared his dream with all the potential partners who might help him carry out his project, beginning with his employer, the long-term care hospital in Baie Comeau.

After many months of research and determination, he finally obtained the financing he needed to create his company.

He hired his old co-worker Marie-Claude as director of human resources and production. "Without her," Claude says, "Norfil could never have existed."

Together they created a unique company that manufactures industrial clothing and protective gear, *Norfil Clothing*.

Their mission is to foster the employability of people with functional limitations. Three quarters of the personnel have such limitations. The other quarter is composed of managers and attendants.

The employees are people who, according to current social norms, would be excluded from the labor force and compelled to rely on the State. Instead, today, they have a trade, earn a living, receive a decent salary and pay taxes.

The quality of the clothes they manufacture is impressive. The stitching is impeccable, the cuts perfect, the finishing irreproachable.

I was astonished to discover a level of quality rarely seen on the market, and even less so for industrial clothing.

The workplace was clean, well lit and pleasant. From our first meetings, the smiles and faces were sympathetic. Everyone seemed focused and attentive to what they were doing. The atmosphere was calm. I felt good there at once.

Several employees told me that the job had changed their lives. Now, they're happy to get up in the morning because they have somewhere to go and something important and useful to do.

The attainment of autonomy translates into a new dignity and respect in the eyes of others. Some of them have their own cars, apartments and live a relatively normal life. The dream of one man succeeded in saving the lives of these people whom society had cast aside.

I was immediately struck by the fact that this team was getting better treatment than most employees in so-called normal companies. The management team knows that without the trust of its troops it could do nothing.

The company relies on a quality support system. There's no question of finding the lowest common denominator here; rather, they are always trying to raise the bar. It's a collective project. Successes are celebrated as a team, and everyone's contribution is recognized.

It's immediately obvious that these people enjoy working together. I was both fascinated and moved.

Companies should take inspiration from this model.

If people with limitations manage to produce such quality, at competitive prices, while respecting human beings and the environment, why do we sometimes fail to do the same with people without so-called limitations?

In fact, we may be the ones with the greatest limitations, simply because our hearts are hardened. We should be wary of our prejudices.

"I find it enriching to work with them; they teach us a wonderful lesson in life," the seamstresses told me. They're right. The few hours I spent with them, I was deeply touched.

In their presence, our artifices and masks fall away. Authenticity is contagious. In short, if I needed to have some industrial clothing manufactured, I'd be happy to associate with such a team.

I'd even be willing to pay the shipping costs, no matter where I was based, because Norfil offers what few other companies can: a very high quality product, made to measure, at a competitive price, along with a human and social conscience, and with compassion. Dealing with them, you have the sense that you're contributing a little bit to the beauty of the world. To its dignity.

I was so impressed I thought Norfil should have a waiting list of potential clients (this is not the case) and partners to open other modified workplaces in its image. It is possible to do better, and Norfil is eloquent proof of that.

Yet, they have to struggle on a fiercely competitive terrain. More and more companies take bids over the Internet, and award contracts to the lowest bidder, regardless of the conditions in which the clothes are manufactured. Anything for profit. And sometimes, the difference is only a few hundred dollars.

What's happening to us? Mega-companies need mega-profits to survive. Aren't we — who consume the products of those mega-companies and contribute to their mega-profits — also responsible for this decline?

We can do something positive, without even impoverishing ourselves, and without losing quality or productivity. Yet, we refuse!

Acts of Beauty

Claude Belzile's dream (and his perseverance in attaining it and keeping it going) is a fine example for us all. An example that ought to make us think twice about how we choose our suppliers.

It's one humanist wager that paid off. By creating Norfil, Claude provided us with an uplifting act of beauty but, more than that, he encourages those around him to do the same, every day.

One person. One dream. One act. And hundreds of other people touched by his grace, dignity and compassion; hundreds of others for whom life has improved. In the name of everyone, thank you, Claude. Thank you Marie-Claude. Thanks to all those who are ready to make one small gesture to build the City, and refuse to let profit become our god to the point of losing our reason. And our hearts.

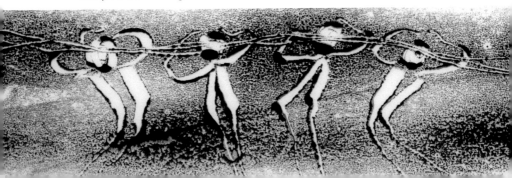

BEAUTY - THIRD ACT

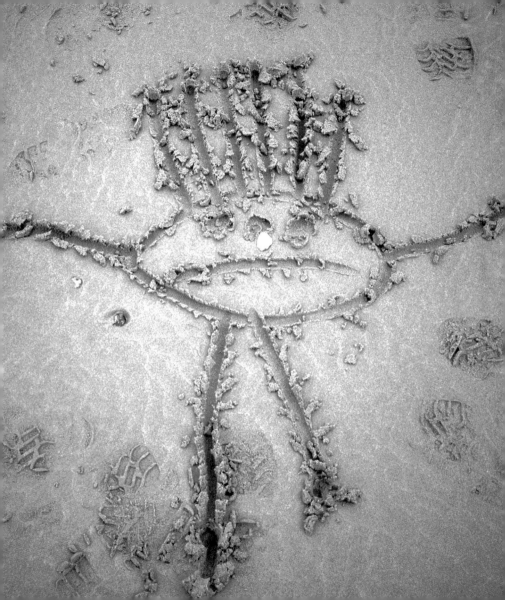

Bringing children into the world is a very serious act. Giving them life is a small thing compared with the quality of support we will give them in the years to come.

Unfortunately, many children — who never asked to be born — come into the world in the most squalid conditions. It's the duty of all of us to join forces to help them.

I personally have a great dream. I'm not in a position to realize it right now, but I'm certain I will one day. For those children I want to help in my way, I intend to put aside a quarter of my annual income, beginning as soon as I can, for the rest of my life.

Until that time, I help a little, but really I'm still at the stage of dreaming and searching for a concept that meets the spirit of my collective intelligence and artistic creation approach. The period of incubation is useful.

I've been working on it in silence and alone for several years now. I want to take time to find the act, among all the possible acts, that will give meaning to my life, and provide lasting benefits to humanity and humanism.

Walter Benjamin wrote that "the origin does not point toward the becoming of what is born, but designates what is in the process of birth, in becoming and also within decline. The origin is a whirlpool in the river of becoming and, into its rhythm, it pulls the material of whatever is in the process of appearing."[16]

I thus hold the hope that, since this desire is already in me, it will find its way to realization in the future, since its origin already exists in my imagination and heart. Which is, as Saint Augustine might say, in the present.

Such was my thinking in the fall of 2002, when Thérèse Dion talked to me about the little boy in India whom she was sponsoring. Immediately, I too wanted to sponsor a child.

Since then, I've been lucky to sponsor Vara Lakshmi, a six-year old girl who's lost her mother, and whom I hope to visit someday.

The fairy godmother behind the orphanage in Puri, India, who allows us to sponsor the children by donating an annual sum to pay for their lodging, food and medical expenses, as well as their education, is Mary-Ellen Gerber.

In 1977, this American woman dedicated part of her fortune to create the Mary-Ellen Gerber Foundation. In May 2000, the Foundation purchased eight acres of land to build the first village for orphans, in Orissa County, Bay of Bengal.

The village now harbors 99 children. The second village, in Visakhapatnam, is home to 25 girls.

These young orphans at last have the hope for a better life. The children help each other, with only a few grandmothers living there to take care of them. New arrivals are warmly welcomed by the older residents.

Several retired people spend time in the villages to teach the children to read and write. I can't describe it fully, because I haven't been yet, but you can visit the website www.megfoundation.org if you're interested in learning more.

Once again, one person. One dream. One act. And the lives of thousands of people have been touched. Mary-Ellen is a multiplier of beauty. Think of all those little children who will have better lives, thanks to her act and all the others it engenders.

In the spring of 2003, I received little Vara's photograph. She is beautiful. I can't wait to meet her.

If she wants to study, I intend to assist her as best I can for as long as possible. And who knows… I may take others under my wing.

When I showed her picture to a friend, Garry Bourgeois, he told me it was not only important to him to help just one child, but to also help them get as far as university. I discovered that this 47-year-old bachelor was the godfather of a little boy (the son of a fellow worker). When the child was born, his gift was the promise to pay the child's college fees. As the mayor of Rome, Walter Veltroni, recently reminded us, if each one of us could save a single life it would already make a huge difference. What's fabulous is that, in talking about one person's act of beauty, we discover others. It's confirmation that humans can also be good and the humanist cause is not impossible.

Paris, Montreal, April-May, 2003

THE GATES OF DESIRE

"But when, despite their suffering, someone murmurs a desire, all that's needed is for another to hear it and the embers again burst into flame."[1]

Boris Cyrulnik

7

For several months I'd felt the urge to be silent. To shrink into my shell. It was as though I'd been overcome by a powerful lassitude that sapped all the strength I might have had to try to convince. Anyway, can we really convince those who act in bad faith?

To put in my two cents worth, but not just add to the general noise… to go beyond giving ineffective speeches in front of audiences who are half asleep. What, in any case, can we say to those who no longer know how to hear?

I'd told all my friends and clients I was taking a break to write, but the more the weeks passed, the more I feared I would be unable to do it.

It was as though I were in a thick fog, looking for lights in the distance to guide me. But the light came from within. The "I" came easily, but it was constraining. An essay would have been less demanding than such an intimate memoir. What's more,

I really felt like writing stories. I had this great desire, and still do, to let myself be swept up by the magic of invented worlds. The imaginary is my country. But I knew that I would first have to pass through this intermediary stage. This stage of reality. I had to cross the threshold of the real to enter the unreal. This threshold was, for me, at once an alchemical process and a synthesis. And it seemed to me I owed this synthesis to the readers of *City of Intelligences*.

Time, too, was pressing. In four years, I'd be fifty years old. I was suddenly afraid of the passage of time. Afraid of having let my dreams pass me by. Afraid of having neglected the causes close to my heart. Driven by this feeling of imminent death, I thought I had to dare to act quickly. In my case, to act meant to stop. To take stock. And to follow Seneca's advice, to know from whence I'd come to try to know where to go. "There's no favorable wind for those who do not know where they are going."

As you can see, my desire to make a better world is still strong. But the point is not merely to dream of a perfect world — that would be a waste of time and, all things considered, possibly quite boring — but rather to put the world to good use.

This is the era of performance at all cost but, in some areas, we aren't performing any more at all.

We should follow the example of the philosophy of the Kanak people of New Caledonia: "For us, our country is sharing... Prestige comes not from capitalizing on resources but from services we render others... In our system, Man is not the master; he's one element in the world."[2]

How could we, with our intelligence, our knowledge and our technical means, have strayed so far from a wisdom that seems so sensible and logical?

Words have rarely had so little meaning. We play with words as though they were fashions. Once the trend is gone, the word emptied of its meaning has lost all substance.

It's high time to give value back to words. We must act. Build before it's too late. Talk will no longer suffice; we must do. **Each act counts.**

It's for the sake of all those threatened by such despair that we must act. It's for them that we must pursue an ideal.

Let's not be cynical, and look down from the height of our certainties and condescension (playing at being the one who knows the way) in the face of what seems naïve to us — but which is often troubling.

I am certain of nothing, but I'd like to try, to give it a try. I can already see us more or less groping our way forward, all together, in the joyful imperfection of our collective creativity. In spite of our doubts.

The older I get, the more I feel the way is unclear. The day I realized this, it saddened me a little.

It was as though I'd set out on a walk in the sun, but the sky suddenly clouded over and the downpour caught me before I could take cover.

As soon as I become overconfident, a new vision appears, as if to make me doubt myself. I move from clear skies to fog, like on those uncertain days when the sun dallies with the clouds.

I hesitate. I'm not sure whether I'm advancing or stepping backward. A passionate nature throws herself into an adventure with everything she has, and is. Such natures require a double dose of wisdom to admit their errors.

When we've invested everything in a cause, it's difficult to admit that we were wrong. And yet, that's life. We make mistakes, from time to time.

Like Peter Brook, "I believe that all life is a progression toward the realization that things are never quite what we think we see, nor what we think we understand."[3]

In the quest for that realization, we often find ourselves stumbling between intuition and doubt, searching for clues and markers to better understanding.

Whenever we see an intuition confirmed or a dream realized, we sense the latent state of things.

That's what I would like us to experience in our collective adventure: the latent state of a stimulating world to invent.

But to achieve this, we may have to return to our childhood, return to the very source of our creativity.

The waking dream reveals our intuitions. I don't know if it's because, as a child, I was allowed to daydream as much as I liked, or because of the powerful effect reading Andersen's *Little Match Girl* had on me. But, as soon as that poor girl struck a match, I was right there with her in the midst of her vision.

That's how I invented myself throughout my childhood, with rites of passage from one level of reality to another. Thanks to a lot of practice, I became quite adept in creating imaginary films for which I was the only audience.

This naïve intuition of childhood convinced me beyond doubt that my thoughts could produce a far more exciting life than the one adults talked about.

Soon, I began to rely heavily on reverie as a mode of existence, to project myself into universes where I directed the action according to my desires.

However, my fertile imagination had one big weakness, which caused me many disappointments: impatience. As soon as I had fine-tuned my visions, they seemed so real that I couldn't understand why they weren't immediately transformed into reality.

This frustration was the source of my taste for action and the desire to share my dreams. For them to become real, others had to believe in them. How could it be otherwise? Stories and dreams were real. It bothered me that others could doubt this. My convictions led me to breathe the marvelous into the dull parts of my life. There was no question of being satisfied with ordinary reality.

I gained a better understanding of my childhood behavior when I read an article by Boris Cyrulnik, explaining "that children that don't dream their future are condemned to live in the present, and can never satisfy their desires. Pity those who have never lied, and are condemned to reality."[4]

Adolescence gave wings to my dreams, occasionally allowing me to enact them as though the magic were real. I had many experiences that strangely resembled my dreams. I remember those euphoric moments when I had the feeling that the imaginary and reality had melded. They thrilled me and gave me complete confidence in life.

Gradually, with the passage of time, my obligations ate away my time for dreaming. Long bus and subway rides, so ideal for mental escapes, were replaced by rapid and often stressful car rides.

The greatest benefit of my childhood belief was to engrave my desires so deeply that, for several years, my actions were driven by enormous passion and enthusiasm. It gave me the tremendous energy that comes from the pursuit of dreams and the desire to achieve them. There's such a joy in seeing what seemed impossible come true. But sometimes life takes so long to align with our spirit that we start to doubt that our dreams will ever be attained. That's when we despair. We end up forgetting or abandoning them — until the day they reappear, which can be frightening, because we suddenly come face to face with our youthful determination that led us to believe we could control our lives and future. That led us to believe everything was possible.

"Nothing seems more intimately familiar to Man than those hopes and desires he has long nourished and kept in his heart. Then when the time comes and they appear before him, imposing themselves on him," writes Goethe, "he fails to recognize them and retreats before them."[5]

When we rely solely on logic we lose touch with the imagination. Yet the imagination is our most powerful key to building reality and, ironically, to developing a logic which provides coherence between our desires, our acts and our lives. We ought to mix Oriental and Western wisdom to surpass our habitual knowledge and thereby arrive at a richer and more mysterious understanding.

What I seek is to find a balance between the immanence that allows my true desires to emerge, and the movement required to attempt to make them happen. Like François Cheng's character, I never stop repeating to myself: "While there's time, it's probably my only chance to make that gesture I so desired, that one gesture that I know I was born to make. And yet, I won't make it right away, knowing full well that if there's still time, this is not yet the time to make it. Isn't that the story of my whole life, never in time, and always bad timing? My life never takes place in a visible and predictable present. It is constantly deferred, for the sake of some hypothetical future achievement. Hypothetical? Well, not entirely. Deep inside, I'm convinced. Forever destitute and dispossessed, I have learned to be sure of nothing, yet I maintain the naïve and indestructible belief that any seed I plant, even if it's no more than a thought or desire, will come to term, and flourish at some point in time, maybe near, maybe far — maybe in another life? — when I least expect it. My main task will rather be to learn to recognize those points in time. If I fail, too bad for me; everything will come to pass anyway, without me."[6]

My reflections came from the dizziness of going faster and faster and trying to constantly perform better (so as to be liked and recognized), to earn more money (so as to spend more), to be always busy (so as to have less free time to think).

In the midst of this whirlwind, only half-conscious, I suddenly realized that I had ceased to dream and that life must have more to offer.

When you come from modest beginnings, you can make the mistake of equating accomplishment with possessions. One day, you realize that's not enough.

Whether we are rich or poor, the loss of dreams seems to me to be a terrible impoverishment that jeopardizes all of society. It's a danger I felt in my own case, at least.

From self-doubt to self-doubt, and with the loss of those dear to me who had brought freedom and tenderness to my childhood, I found myself face to face with myself, surprised to discover I no longer knew my true desires and, above all, I no longer knew what to dream.

My summer break helped me to see more clearly. My desires resurfaced, my reveries found the space they needed to roam freely through my life again, and my nights became peopled with dreams.

At times I was afraid I wouldn't fulfill my promise, but here I am, writing the last lines like someone setting the table for guests. Dreamers, thinkers, creators, actors will soon pass through the doors of my desires, so that something beautiful can happen.

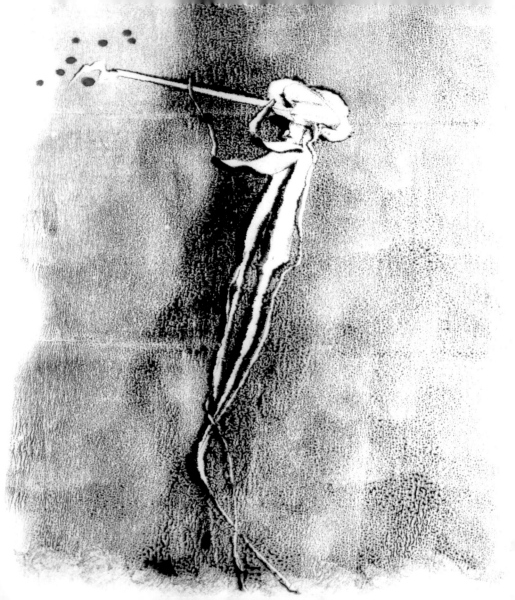

If we can answer the call, if we have the creative strength to show all the beauty that already exists in the world, and the beauty we will invent, then perhaps we can intervene in the destiny of those who leave us prematurely out of despair. They might stay with us a little longer if we invited them to dream and create to build a more decent future. A more humane world.

If you share the same dream as I do, and you decide to act to make a small difference, and you want to share your gesture with others, to show us the stone you have added to the edifice of what could become the School of Desires, I invite you to write me at temoignages@gendreau.com.

The third volume of the School of Desires will present these multiple acts of beauty, in order that we might inspire each other, give ourselves hope, and allow us all to see our collective dream take shape, little by little, before our eyes.

A dream come true. If you have this book before you, it's because another dream has been realized. As I was writing, it seemed unlikely that I'd find the funds to publish and make it available to you. I was doing it first of all for myself, taking stock before moving on. But I also wanted to find a way to offer it to those who share my questions, in the hope that what helps me to live might help them too. I saw it as an act of sharing and beauty, intimate and personal. I saw it as a light breeze murmuring in your ear an invitation to dream and to invent the *School of Desires*. Alas, its production, with all the color photographs, was a great risk. That's when I recalled the old Arab proverb: "A man who has never risked losing everything is a poor man." So, I took the risk. I hope it will be useful to your desires. As it has been to mine.

Montreal, November 2003

Acknowledgements. Friendship, for me, is the very expression of beauty. Bonds that show us the ways of sharing, communication, tenderness and solidarity. Bonds that help to educate us as human beings. A continuing and never-ending education. That's why I'd like to thank all my friends for their smiles, their availability, generosity and sincerity. My friends are for me multipliers of beauty.

To speak of dreams and beauty is a perilous enterprise at a time when these words have become clichés, robbed of their meanings, their depth and their complexity. I took the risk because I believe there are more of us than we might think who would prefer a different discourse, more balanced and more respectful of others.

Thanks also to all those readers who gave me their generous comments before publication: André, Brigitte, Claudette, Jean-François, Jean-Guy, Jovette, Louis, Marc, Michel(s),

Michelle and Nicole(s). Thanks to my proof-readers: Michel Durand, Wendy Gardner, Nadine Li Lung Hok. And a very special one to my talented translators Robert Majzels and Erin Moure.

Thanks to all those whose paths crossed mine these last few months, and who helped me to create this book of personal reflections, or rather this game to ask for your help so that we might do our best to protect the beauty of this world.

Picasso once said to Jean Cocteau: "We must create beyond beauty, because if we merely attempt to reproduce beauty, we end up with no more than a pastiche. If we go beyond it, beauty will catch up with our creation."[1] It's what I wish for all of us in our future creations.

Montreal, June 2004

NOTES

* indicates translation into English by Majzels and Mouré

1. ESCAPE FROM REALITY

1. Marc de Smedt, *Zen, les carnets de la sagesse [Zen, Notebooks of Wisdom]*, Paris: Albin Michel.*

2. Michel Random and Hélène Barrère, *La vision transpersonnelle et la psychologie holistique [Transpersonal Vision and Holistic Psychology]*, Éditions Dervy, 1996, p.19.*

3. Gaston Bachelard, *The Poetics of Reverie*, trans. Daniel Russell, New York: The Orion Press, 1969, p. 5.

4. Régis Debray, *Par amour de l'art, une éducation intellectuelle [For Love of Art, an Intellectual Education]*, Paris: Éditions Gallimard, 1998, p. 27.*

5. Harry N. Abrams, *Modigliani l'inconnu : collection de dessins de Paul Alexandre [The Unknown Modigliani: Drawings from the Collection of Paul Alexandre]*, catalogue, Musée du Luxembourg, 1993.*

6. Italo Calvino, *Leçons américaines [American Lessons]*, Paris: Éditions du Seuil, Point, 2001, p. 147.*

7. Ibid, p. 147.

8. Ibid, p. 149.

9. René Lenoir, *Repères pour les hommes d'aujourd'hui [Guidelines for Men Today]*, Paris: Fayard, 1998, p. 83.*

10. Cyrille J.-D. Javardy, Pierre Faure, *Yi Jing*, Paris: Albin Michel, 2002, p. 25.*

11. Pablo Neruda, *Memoirs*, trans. Hardie St. Martin, New York: Farrar Strauss and Giroux, 2001, p. 269.

12. Boris Cyrulnik, *Un merveilleux malheur [A Marvelous Misfortune]*, Éditions Odile Jacob, 1999, p. 18.*

13. Nicolas Truong, "Entretien avec Antonio Negri. La vie est une prison quand on ne la construit pas [Interview with Antonio Negri. Life is a Prison When We Do Not Build It]," Le Monde de L'éducation, June, 2002.*

14. Michel Lacroix, "Les modèles du moi [Models of the Self]," *Magazine Psychologie*, September, 2002.*

2. THE DREAM'S SHARE

1. Gilles Vigneault, *L'armoire des jours [The Cabinet of Days]*, Nouvelles éditions de l'arc, Montreal, Quebec, 1998, p. 109.*

2. Honoré de Balzac, *La comédie humaine [The Human Comedy]*, Éditions Jean de Bonnot, Paris, p. vii.*

3. Carl Jung, *Psychology and Alchemy, The Collected Works of Carl Jung*, Vol. 12, trans. R.F.C. Hull, Princeton: Princeton University Press, 4th printing, 1977, p. 8.

4. Kim Masters, "The Last Emperors," *Vanity Fair*, September, 1999.

5. Armand Mattelart, *Histoire de l'utopie planétaire [The History of Planetary Utopia]*, Éditions de la découverte, 1999.*

6. Carl Jung, *Psychology and Alchemy, The Collected Works of Carl Jung*, Vol. 12, trans. R.F.C. Hull, Princeton: Princeton University Press, 4th printing, 1977, p. 31.

7. Edgar Morin, "Imaginer le futur [Imagining the Future]," *Les clés du XXe siècle [Keys to the 20th Century]*, Paris: Éditions du Seuil, Éditions Unesco, April, 2000, p. 61.*

8. Alain Berthoz, *The Brain's Sense of Movement,* trans. Giselle Weiss, Boston: Harvard University Press, 2000, p. 6.

9. Thierry Gaudin, *2100, Récit du prochain siècle [2100, The Story of the Next Century],* Paris: Grande Bibliothèque, Payot, 1990, p. 7.*

10. Ibid, p. 7.*

11. Luc Perreault, "On ne communique plus, déplore Scola [We No Longer Communicate, Scola Deplores]," *La Presse,* Montreal, September 5, 1999.*

12. Jean-Pierre Kreif, *La Rage et le rêve des condamnés [The Rage and the Dream of the Condemned]*, 20th International Art Film Festival, Montreal, 2002.

3. THE ROAD OF DESIRES

1. François Cheng, *Le dit de Tianyi [The Story of Tianyi],* Paris: Albin Michel, 1998, p. 57.*

2. Lao-Tseu, Tao Tö King, *Le livre de la voie et de la vertu*, Traduction de Conradin Von Lauer, Jean de Bonnot, Paris, 2002, p. 2*

3. Ibid, p.3.

4. Jean Giono, *L'oiseau bagué, L'imaginaire [The Ringed Bird, Imagination]*, Paris: Éditions Gallimard, 1943, p. 15.*

5. Christian Bobin, *Autoportrait du radiateur [Self-portrait of the Radiator]*, Paris: Éditions Gallimard, 1997, p. 17.*

6. Gérard Macé, *Colportage 1, Lectures, Le promeneur [Gossip Mongering 1, Readings, The Stroller]*, Paris: Éditions Gallimard, 1998, p. 13.*

7. Alain Vicondelet, *Saint-Exupéry, Vérité et légendes [Saint Exupéry, Truth and Legends]*, Éditions du Chêne, Hachette, 2000, p. 107.*

8. Peter Brook, *Le diable c'est l'ennui [The Devil is Boredom]*, Paris: Actes Sud-papiers, 1991, p. 13.*

9. Pietro Citati, *La lumière de la nuit, les grands mythes dans l'histoire du monde [The Light in the Night, Great Myths in the History of the World]*, L'Arpenteur, Paris: Éditions Gallimard, 1999, p. 122.*

10. Jean-Pierre Denis, *"Vivre c'est avoir peur [To Live is To Be Afraid]"*, Le Devoir, Montreal, Quebec, April 30, 2000.*

11. Zaki Laïdi, *La tyrannie de l'urgence [The Tyranny of Urgency]*, Les Grandes conférences, Éditions Fides, 1999, p. 32.*

12. François Cheng, *Le dit de Tianyi [The Story of Tianyi]*, Paris: Albin Michel, 1998, p.124.*

13. Ibid.

14. Ibid.

15. J. W. von Goethe, *Wilhelm Meister's Apprenticeship*, Vol. XIV, Harvard Classics Shelf of Fiction, New York: P.F. Collier & Son, 1917; Bartleby.com, 2000.

4. DREAMWEAVERS

1. Milan Kundera, *The Joke,* trans. copyright Harper Collins (Heim, revised by Kundera) London: Faber and Faber, 1992, p. 226.

2. Sebastião Salgado, *"Pouvons-nous réconcilier la planète des hommes? [Can We Reconcile the Planet of Men?],"* Interview in *L'Express,* Paris, March 2000.*

3. Ibid.*

4. Ibid.*

5. Michel Maffesoli, *L'instant éternel, le retour du tragique dans les sociétés postmodernes [The Eternal Instant, Return of the Tragic in Postmodern Societies],* Paris: Denoël, 2000, p. 53.*

6. Serge Bouchard, *"Sale histoire [Dirty Story],"* *Le Devoir,* Monday, July 31, 2000.*

7. Gilles Vigneault, *L'armoire des jours [The Cabinet of Days],* Montreal, Quebec: Nouvelles éditions de l'arc, 1998, p. 83.*

8. J. W. von Goethe. *Wilhelm Meister's Apprenticeship,* Vol. XIV, Harvard Classics Shelf of Fiction, New York: P.F. Collier & Son, 1917; Bartleby.com, 2000.

9. Ibid.*

10. Ibid.*

11. Jacques Attali, *Fraternités [Fraternities],* Paris: Fayard, 1999, p. 57.*

12. G. Lakoff, "How Metaphor Structures Dreams: The Theory of Conceptual Metaphor Applied to Dream Analysis," *Dreaming*, Vol. 3, No. 77, 1993.

13. Italo Calvino, *Leçons américaines [American Lessons]*, Paris: Éditions du Seuil, Point, 2001, p. 70.*

14. Saint Augustine, *Confessions*, trans. and ed. by Albert C. Outler, 1955, scanned by Harry Plantinga, whp@wheaton.edu 1994, p. 164.

15. Andrew Newberg, Eugene D'Aquili, Vince Rause, *Why God Won't Go Away: Brain Science and the Biology of Belief*, New York: Ballantine Books, April 2001, p. 32.

5. BOREAL MEDITATIONS

1. Jean Desy, *La rêverie du froid [Reverie of Cold]*, Quebec City: Le Palindrome, Les éditions de la liberté, 1991, p. 82.*

2. George Steiner, *Errata: An Examined Life*, London: Weidenfeld & Nicholson, 1997, p. 5.

3. Yves Simon, *La dérive des sentiments [The Drift of Feelings]*, Livre de poche, Paris: Grasset, 1991, p. 52.*

4. René Lenoir, *Repères pour les hommes d'aujourd'hui [Guidelines for Men Today]*, Paris: Fayard, 1998, p. 200.*

5. Ibid, p. 69.*

6. Jean-Louis Bernard, "Création artistique et dynamique d'insertion, *Colloque transnational* [Artistic Creation and the Dynamics of Insertion]," *Transnational Colloquium*, Paris: Éditions L'Harmattan, 2001, p. 10.*

7. Ibid, p. 12-13.*

8. Jean Desy, *La rêverie du froid [Reverie of Cold]*, Quebec City: Le Palindrome, Les éditions de la liberté, 1991, p. 77.*

9. Milan Kundera, *The Joke,* trans. copyright Harper Collins (Heim, revised by Kundera) London: Faber and Faber, 1992, p. 175-6.

10. Yves Simon, *La dérive des sentiments [The Drift of Feelings]*, Livre de poche, Paris: Éditions Grasset, 1991, p. 179.*

11. Giovanni Maciocia, *Les principes de la médecine chinoise [Principles of Chinese Medicine]*, Brussels: Satas, 1992, p. 9, cited by Cajetan Larochelle, in *Socrate, sage et guerrier [Socrates, Sage and Warrior]*, Montreal: Éditions Intouchables, 1999.*

12. Pascal Bruckner, *L'euphorie perpétuelle, essai sur le devoir du bonheur [Perpetual Euphoria, Essay on the Duty of Happiness]*, Paris: Grasset, 2000, p. 182.*

13. Carla Bruni, "L'excessive [The Excessive]," CD: *Quelqu'un m'a dit [Someone Told Me]*, 2003.*

14. Michel Maffesoli, *L'instant éternel, le retour du tragique dans les sociétés postmodernes [The Eternal Instant, Return of the Tragic in Postmodern Societies]*, Paris: Denoël, 2000, p. 97.*

15. Pascal Bruckner, *L'euphorie perpétuelle, essai sur le devoir du bonheur [Perpetual Euphoria, Essay on the Duty of Happiness]*, Paris: Grasset, 2000, p. 52.*

16. Michel Maffesoli, *L'instant éternel, le retour du tragique dans les sociétés postmodernes [The Eternal Instant, Return of the Tragic in Postmodern Societies]*, Paris: Denoël, 2000, p. 190.*

17. Jean Hurstel, "Huit thèses et une synthèse sur la question de l'art et de l'insertion [Eight Theses and One Synthesis on the Question of Art and Insertion]," *Transnational Colloquium*, Paris: Éditions L'Harmattan, 2001, p. 48.*

18. Cornelius Castoriadis, *La montée de l'insignifiance, les carrefours du labyrinthe [The Rise of Insignificance, the Crossroads of the Labyrinth]*, Paris: Éditions du Seuil, 1996, p. 63.*

6. ACTS OF BEAUTY

1. Dominique Fernandez, *La beauté [Beauty]*, Desclée de Brouwer & Shanghai Literary and Artistic Press, 2000, p. 127.*

2. Cyrille J.-D. Javardy, Pierre Faure, *Yi Jing*, Paris: Albin Michel, 2002, p. 29.*

3. Italo Calvino, *Leçons américaines [American Lessons]*, Paris: Éditions du Seuil, Point, 2001, p. 57.*

4. Dominique Fernandez, *La beauté [Beauty]*, Desclée de Brouwer & Shanghai Literary and Artistic Press, 2000, p. 86.*

5. Hubert Reeves, *La synchronicité, l'âme et la science [Synchronicity, the Soul and Science]*, Paris: Espaces libres, Albin Michel, 1995, p. 19.*

6. Milan Kundera, *The Joke*, trans. copyright Harper Collins (Heim, revised by Kundera) London: Faber and Faber, 1992, p. 164.

7. Hubert Reeves, *La synchronicité, l'âme et la science [Synchronicity, the Soul and Science]*, Paris: Espaces libres, Albin Michel, 1995, p. 19.*

8. Michel Maffesoli, *L'instant éternel, le retour du tragique dans les sociétés postmodernes [The Eternal Instant, Return of the Tragic in Postmodern Societies]*, Paris: Denoël, 2000, p. 103.*

9. Ibid, p. 103.*

10. George Steiner, *Errata: An Examined Life*, London: Weidenfeld & Nicholson, 1997, p.170-171.

11. Tzvetan Todorov, *Le jardin imparfait : la pensée humaniste en France [The Imperfect Garden: Humanist Thought in France]*, Paris: Grasset, 1998, p. 327.*

12. Jean Hurstel, "*Huit thèses et une synthèse sur la question de l'art et de l'insertion [Eight Theses and One Synthesis on the Question of Art and Insertion]*," Transnational Colloquium, Éditions L'Harmattan, 2001, p. 48.*

13. Tzvetan Todorov, *Le jardin imparfait : la pensée humaniste en France [The Imperfect Garden: Humanist Thought in France]*, Paris: Grasset, 1998, pp. 331-332.*

14. Roland Barthes, *Oeuvres complètes [Complete Works]*, vol. III, Paris: Éditions du Seuil, p. 398.*

15. Rima Elkouri, "Bernard le concierge [Bernard the Janitor]," *La Presse*, Montreal, Quebec, May 9, 2003.*

16. Cyrille J.-D. Javardy, Pierre Faure, *Yi Jing*, Paris: Albin Michel, 2002, p. 23.*

7. THE GATES OF DESIRE

1. Boris Cyrulnik, *Le murmure des fantômes [The Murmur of Ghosts]*, Éditions Odile Jacob, 2003, p. 236.*

2. Jean-Marie Tjibaou, *La présence kanak [The Kanak Presence]*, Éditions Odile Jacob, 1997.*

3. Peter Brook, *Avec Shakespeare [Evoking Shakespeare]*, Arles: Actes Sud-papiers, 1998, p. 61.*

4. Boris Cyrulnik, "La mythomanie est fondatrice de notre destin [Mythomania is the Foundation of our Destiny]," *Magazine Psychologie*, September 2002.*

5. J. W. von Goethe. *Wilhelm Meister's Apprenticeship*, Vol. XIV, Harvard Classics Shelf of Fiction, New York: P.F. Collier & Son, 1917; Bartleby.com, 2000.

6. François Cheng, *Le dit de Tianyi [The Story of Tianyi]*, Paris: Albin Michel, 1998, p.187.*

8. ACKNOWLEDGEMENTS

1. Jean-Paul Fargier (Director), *Cocteau & Compagnie,* French Movie, 2003 (52 min.) presented at the 22nd Festival International du Film sur l'Art, Montréal 2004.

Designed by
Gendreau Communications Graphics
Printed in September 2004
by Litho-Milles-Îles ltée
for Éditions Céra, Montréal